Sylvia Smith

**Letters Across
the Divide**

Thank you for being
a Bridgebuilder
And for your heart
for reconcilation!

Most of all, thanks for
Listening & supporting
"Reconcilation Live"!

1/07

Letters Across the Divide

Two Friends Explore Racism, Friendship, and Faith

David Anderson & Brent Zuercher

Baker Books

A Division of Baker Book House Co
Grand Rapids, Michigan 49516

Published by Baker Books
a division of Baker Book House Company
P.O. Box 6287, Grand Rapids, MI 49516-6287

Printed in the United States of America

Library of Congress Cataloging-in-Publication Data

Anderson, David, 1966–
    Letters across the divide : two friends explore racism, friendship, and faith /
David Anderson & Brent Zuercher.
        p.   cm.
    Includes bibliographical references and index.
    ISBN 0-8010-6343-4 (paper)
        1. Race relations—Religious aspects—Christianity. 2. Reconciliation—
Religious aspects—Christianity. 3. Anderson, David, 1966—Correspondence.
4. Zuercher, Brent—Correspondence. 5. Christians—United States—Correspondence. I. Zuercher, Brent. II. Title.
BT734.2.A53   2001
261.8′348′00973—dc21

00-063081

Scripture quotations marked NIV are taken from the HOLY BIBLE, NEW INTERNATIONAL VERSION®. NIV®. Copyright © 1973, 1978, 1984 by International Bible Society. Used by permission of Zondervan Publishing House. All rights reserved.

Scripture quotations marked NKJV are taken from the New King James Version. Copyright © 1979, 1980, 1982 by Thomas Nelson, Inc. Used by permission. All rights reserved.

Scripture quotations marked KJV are taken from the King James Version of the Bible.

The authors express appreciation for permission to reprint:

"Blessed Are the Peacemakers." This article first appeared in the June 1994 issue of *Moody* Magazine. It is reprinted with permission.

"For Many Blacks, Simpson Case Is, Indeed, about Race" by Clarence Page. © Tribune Media Services, Inc. All rights reserved. Reprinted with permission.

"Southern Baptists Approve Apology for Longtime Racism." Reprinted with permission of the Associated Press.

"Southern Baptists Offer an Apology." Copyright 1995, *USA Today*. Reprinted with permission.

On pages 65–66, excerpt from "Blinded by the White," by Ray Hartman, Nov. 5, 1997, *The Riverfront Times*.

For current information about all releases from Baker Book House, visit our web site:
http://www.bakerbooks.com

Contents

Prologue

A Note to the Reader from David

*I*n recent years there has been an increasing focus within the church on racial reconciliation. The mere fact that you are reading this reveals that you are at least mildly curious about what racial reconciliation is really all about and what implications it has for your life. There are many ways of approaching this emotionally charged topic and as the senior pastor of a multicultural church, I have seen my congregation use several. The least effective is of course a lecture where the speaker presents his perspective and the audience passively listens and then goes home. The most effective way of dealing with the many facets of racial reconciliation is through individual relationships among members of different races. Whether it is in a small group or a one-on-one between two people, some form of personal interaction is essential.

I am committed to consistently lifting up the core value of racial reconciliation before my congregation. This is a significant part of my everyday life. I understand, though, that not everyone has my same level of interest or devotion to this issue. You may have little commitment to racial reconciliation but perhaps just a seed of interest. My hope is that by allowing you to essentially eavesdrop on a written conversation between a close personal friend of mine and me, the seed within you will be watered and Christ will grow that seed as He consistently draws you to Himself and toward others.

Before you read on, I think it would be helpful if you understood the context in which the following conversation took place. I am African American and Brent is white. We first met at the singles group I was pastoring as an intern at a large predominately white church in the northwest suburbs of Chicago. Our acquaintance turned into a friendship through the experience of the small group. As friends, we laughed together, prayed together, played basketball together, worshiped together, served together, and talked too late into the night. We know the dirt on each other, we appreciate the strengths of each other, and we genuinely enjoy each other's company.

On completing my internship, I moved from Chicago to Columbia, Maryland, to plant a multicultural church. Brent is a certified public accountant and through our friendship he had demonstrated that he was a person I could trust. Therefore I asked Brent to help me get the church started in the right direction fiscally and legally. Brent agreed to be our treasurer but not to relocate from Chicago. One of the reasons he decided not to move to Columbia was that he had unresolved issues and unanswered questions about race. As a result, during Bridgeway Community Church's infancy, Brent and I corresponded, addressing his questions and issues.

The dialogue you are about to read was our personal and real conversation about race. It reflects our personalities and experiences and is not necessarily the conversation you would have. Personal aspects of our lives were discussed in other conversations, either over the phone or face-to-face. The letters you will read were simply the vehicle we used to discuss this one particular topic. Why did we do this via letters? Since we didn't live in the same town, we couldn't get together and talk, and letters were cheaper than hours and hours and hours of long-distance phone calls. Letters also gave us time to process our responses and write and rewrite our thoughts.

Let me caution you that our conversation is in no way a substitute for the reality of your need to engage in your own conversation with someone of another race. My relational connection with Brent was the foundation of our ability to converse with openness and honesty about such matters. We encourage you to find a safe cross-cultural relationship where you can explore these matters in greater and more personal depth. Do not allow yourself to live vicariously through our conversation, deceiving yourself and thinking that you too have journeyed down the road of reconciliation. The journey is not a vicarious one but must be a personal experience. Our desire is that these letters will inspire you to begin your own journey. You will find questions in the appendix that will assist you in having your own conversation, whether one-on-one or in a small group.

You will notice that some of the letters have footnotes, offering additional guidance or clarification as to what we were thinking when we wrote. Since the time these letters were written, our views on certain points may have changed slightly, so we have also inserted footnotes to amend or offer a more rounded view, without changing the content of the letter as it was originally written.

The reader should feel free to go directly to any letter that interests him or her. The conversation is an ongoing one from beginning to end, but each group of letters is a conversation from beginning to end as well.

Allow me to make this disclaimer at the very beginning. The conversation that Brent and I had is a real one that uses broad statements. We do not see ourselves as the absolute voice for our respective groups, although in the privacy of our conversation from our own experiences and opinions, we may view ourselves as speaking for those groups.

Although we do not need to give the details, from the time Brent and I started our conversation until today there have been bumps and diversions, hard feelings, apologies, and forgiveness—that is part of any relationship and friendship. By the end of the last letter, you will have learned how Brent and I moved along the continuum of racial reconciliation.

I need to make one other point. There are three kinds of racism: individual, institutional, and indirect racism. *Individual racism* is the personal view one holds, affecting people on an individual level. *Institutional racism* is a systemic and sociological condition that creates an environment whereby particular kinds of people are excluded from the positive norms of that institution. *Indirect racism* could be individual, institutional, or the integration of both. However, indirect racism is not a targeted form of racism. It is better described as "neglecting" certain kinds of people from the positive norms of an institution or society as opposed to "creating" an environment of exclusion.

The bulk of Brent's and my conversation is about personal or individual racism. We do touch on the topics of institutional and indirect racism as it is germane to the discussion, but our dialogue is one that honestly struggles through the difficulties of our own experiences.

The start of a conversation

David,

*W*hen you left Chicago three years ago to return to the D.C. area to plant Bridgeway Community Church, I never imagined that one day I would be asking you to take the time to dialogue with me about racism and racial reconciliation. I hesitate to start this conversation, though, because I'm comfortable with our friendship the way it is, I value it, and I do not want to create a rift between us. Yet I also know that, if we do not at some point discuss our individual perspectives on race and racial matters, over time our now growing friendship will no longer grow and will begin to become distant.

The last time we talked you asked what my expectations were for our discussion. It's hard to know what my expectations are. The issue of racism has just never affected me before and it probably wouldn't be affecting me now if I were not intentionally exposing myself to it. I have never been forced to confront the issue because it does not directly affect my daily life. I live in a middle-class, predominately white suburb of Chicago and there are only a couple of minorities in my office. The only occasion I have for encounters with people of different racial origin is riding public transportation from my home to downtown. Clearly, and probably unfortunately, the most significant exposure I have to racial matters is from news media coverage where I am insulated from the realities by either the paper in my hand or the television I'm watching.

Most of America, whether white or black or beige, is probably like me in that they do not consider themselves racist but in reality have not made the honest introspective search of their hearts and souls to be able to defend their actions or lack of action. My hope, and yes maybe my expectation, is that this dialogue will allow us to share thoughts and perspectives from both sides of the coin, and that we will both develop a greater understanding of today's racial issues. But to be honest, I guess I fear that when all is said and done, nothing will have changed in me or in the world around me.

I realize that we are not at the same place along the continuum of racial reconciliation. You were forced to progress a long way in the process before we ever met and you have continued to reconcile, within yourself, the black and white worlds you have lived in. I'd like to hear sometime how you were able to do that, how you were able to serve as a pastoral intern at a large and predominately white church without denying the black cultural part of yourself.

Now, you tell me, what are your expectations?

BZ

Brent,

My dear brother, I understand your fear of nothing changing, and even your fear for our future as friends. But trust me, I expect something to change; I expect you will change. At the very least, your conscience will change knowing that you did what you could to honestly and authentically investigate the issue. Let me assure you here at the start of our discussion that our friendship is deeper and I'm more committed to you than I am to this issue of racial reconciliation.

If I died today, I would be happy with what I have done to inspire oneness and unity regarding this particular issue without making it the paramount purpose of my existence. I can love you as my friend and brother no matter where you are on the continuum of change for racial reconciliation.* Your ability to grow in this area (or any other area) was not a prerequisite, nor an acid test, for our friendship to begin five years ago—and it is not now.

Regarding my time as an intern and student in Chicago, I was able to survive the cultural differences because of my focus, not my needs. I have needs of acceptance within my own community. I have needs for peer support from those who look like me and who socialize like me. I have needs to connect with people whose music and upbringing and styles are similar to mine. However, I didn't focus on my needs. I focused on the needs of those around me, and the mission for which God had called me to in both these environments. In addition, I have come far enough down the continuum of reconciliation to allow me to interact, relate to, and love white people as people, and often brothers and sisters. Because of this I didn't carry a chip on my shoulder about racial issues. However, like evangelism, I tried to use every available opportunity to share knowledge about reconciliation and demonstrate the love of Christ. I truly loved educating whites on issues regarding the black community. And when someone said or did something that was offensive, I would use that incident as a "teaching moment."

DA

David,

*B*efore I get started asking questions I need to acknowledge that some of the questions I'm anticipating asking and some of the statements

---

*I too as a black man recognize my need for personal development as I travel this journey down the road of reconciliation. The perspective that enables me to assist Brent is the intentional struggle that I have engaged in throughout the years.

13

I will make during this discussion will probably offend or even anger you. They may be racist statements or just plain ignorant comments.*

I ask that you extend grace to me when this happens, for my purpose is not to offend but to honestly and vulnerably seek the truth and reconciliation. Perhaps I am wrong but I do not believe the issue of racism in America can honestly or effectively be discussed without the freedom to offend within the bounds of love. The whole issue of racism is offensive, and there may be times when words said here, by either one of us, will be offensive to the other. I commit to you here and now that in the times I am offended by your words, I will extend grace to you. And I commit to you that I will stay in this dialogue with you until we can both affirm that we are indeed well on the road to a lifetime of racial reconciliation with each other.

I also want to extend the offer to you now that if at any time this process hinders our working relationship on the Bridgeway Community Church board, I will step aside from service on the board until such time as we are reconciled with each other. I will not allow what is intended to be a good process to turn into a bad thing for the church.

You should also know that this exercise is in no way an attempt on my part to be another white man trying to appease his conscience and adopt the black cause as my own. Such an objective would be foolish because I do not believe you or even blacks in general desire whites to take up the black cause. I am simply attempting to understand how racial reconciliation and racial issues dovetail with God's specific "cause" and objectives for my life. I want

*The difference between racist statements and ignorant statements is their intent. A statement that appears racist on the surface may reveal a heart or perspective that is racist or may simply reveal ignorance as to what is offensive or racist and may not at all be a true indicator of one's heart or perspective.

to pursue God's cause and God's goals—not man's dreams or desires.

So what do you think? Are we on board together?

BZ

Brent,

Thanks for the warning and your offer to step away from the board if things get too dicey. We are "on board" together and I'll stay with you through it all, even though I am having a hard time picturing you taking the gloves off and throwing punches. On the contrary I am trusting that God will continue to use you in a big way with this ministry in some capacity or another. I am not a prophet who can accurately predict what that role will be but I do know that God has intersected our lives for a greater purpose than either one of us can fully understand. I am fully convinced that God equips us for every good work and has afforded us the wisdom needed to make huge strides for the kingdom. His Spirit will make known to us which direction to take as we approach each intersection. Together we will rest in these truths.

DA

What is racism?

Essential to any conversation is ensuring that everybody is speaking the same language and using that language with commonly understood meanings. Although asking a simple question such as, What is racism? may seem to be elementary and unnecessary because the definition is logical—things are not always what they seem. We were surprised by our differing definitions of racism. But is it really any surprise that two people who have different experiences in life and grew up with differing cultural expectations would approach this polarizing topic with differing definitions of the fundamental issue? We so often assume that others perceive the world as we ourselves perceive it. Racism is no different than any other perception of reality—it is a mistake to assume that the person you are talking to defines the word the same way you do. Before you read our definitions in the following discussion, you may want to mentally solidify your own definition of racism.

———

David,

I thought we'd start with the basics and go from there. There's nothing more basic than defining what racism is and clarifying whether racism still exists at all in our country.

Although it has not always been this way, overt and violent racist behavior, whether conducted by the KKK or an individual, is now considered criminal behavior and is punishable by a significant jail sentence. The discriminatory institutional racism of the Jim Crow laws is no longer a part of America's legal structure. These laws and equal opportunity laws are now so prevalent that it is even illegal for a large employer who says it is an "equal opportunity employer" to exclude pictures of minorities in that company's recruiting brochures when there are pictures of whites. The marches, demonstrations, and civil disobedience of blacks during the civil rights movement and beyond have been successful and have resulted in laws that put all races on the same legal ground. Blacks, and all other minorities, have achieved legal equality in America.

The "white perspective" is that since blacks and all other races now have legal equality with whites, the issue of racism is really a dead issue. The white person not only does not understand why blacks make such a big deal about racism anymore, whites do not even want to discuss the issue because it has been legislated and regulated and therefore "solved" so why talk about a problem that does not even exist. The "black perspective" is that racism is still a major problem that deserves significant attention. Blacks view the lack of desire of whites to discuss racism as being a blatant attempt to deny and suppress the racist that is ingrained in their very nature.

Obviously both perspectives cannot be right because they answer the same question differently, the question of, Does racism still exist in America? However, before we answer that question we should define racism. I would define it as making a judgment or statement or decision based purely on a person's racial origin.

For example*: If a black man, let's call him Robert, is at a party mingling and socializing and he sees two people (one black, one white) standing by the food table, alone, not talking to anyone, not even each other and if Robert decides whom he is going to approach and talk to strictly

---

*This example would underscore individual racism. The difference between individual, institutional, and indirect racism can be found in the prologue.

based on the race of the other person, then Robert's actions are racist, right? It does not matter whether he talks to the black man or the white, if his decision was based strictly on race, his actions were racist. Such behavior by Robert is harmless and nonthreatening to the physical well-being of anyone, but it is still racist. Is this an accurate definition? If not, how would you define racism?

BZ

Brent,

*I*n your last letter, you wrote about a hypothetical character by the name of Robert. I believe your definitions of racism were off the mark in this scenario. If a black man chooses to talk to another black man, instead of another white man, it doesn't necessarily imply racism. It could be described as familiarity, a sense of affinity, or as favoritism, partiality, or maybe just insensitivity. However, if we know the man's motives, background, and thoughts, it could be racism. If Robert neglected the white or black person because of their color and he had negative thoughts and prejudicial presuppositions about the person he was neglecting, then we could classify it as racism.

We must remember that racism has never been primarily a problem of actions that could be legislated or regulated. Actions are merely an indicator of a problem contained deeper in the heart and in the beliefs of a person. Individual racism cannot be changed through legislation but through personal transformation. The civil rights and equal opportunity laws that now exist give African Americans, and other minorities, greater physical safety and for many a means of earning a living. However, just because these laws have reduced the physical expressions of racism, this does not mean that racism is an evil that has been put behind us. Just because the laws of an institution have changed, it doesn't mean that the ways of the institution have changed.

Some expressions of institutional racism can be prosecuted when discovered. Such racism can also be lobbied against in the governmental system, the justice system, the educational system, the media, and even in the corporate marketplace. The laws we've mentioned may even preclude certain expressions of racism. However, finding a way around the civil rights laws is just like getting around tax laws. When a new tax law comes out, a new loophole is invented to maneuver around it. Many times the well-intended civil rights and equal opportunity laws are circumvented by those looking for "loopholes" or ways to satisfy the letter of the law while ignoring the spirit of the law.

Do not be deceived, racism still exists in America, both individual and institutional. Negative thoughts and presuppositions about African Americans are everywhere. The KKK may not be the powerhouse it used to be, but equality and equal opportunity are still elusive and hard to obtain for many minorities.

DA

David,

I am beginning to understand more why the word "racism" is so inflammatory for people of every race. The word eludes a consensus definition, even between us. I must admit though it surprises me that I am arguing for a more comprehensive definition of racism than you are. However, I believe it is important that we agree on some sort of a definition.

Your sentence, "If Robert neglected the white or black person because of their color and he had negative thoughts and prejudicial presuppositions about the person he was neglecting, then we could classify it as racism," is a loaded sentence. I disagree with you. I don't think we have to know anything else about Robert's motives, background, thoughts, or presuppositions to make a determination as to whether Robert's choice was a choice tainted by racism.

To define racism as taking an action or making a choice based solely on another person's race is a very objective standard. Your use of the word "and" in the above sentence changes the definition of racism from an objective definition to a subjective definition. Once the definition becomes subjective, it becomes a moving target. Anyone, white or black, then becomes able to defend his actions or choices as being only tainted in favoritism, partiality, or insensitivity—lesser evils in the sight of man. As long as we can justify away our racism as being favoritism, then we don't need to seek reconciliation, and racial unity will continue to elude the church.

"Racism" as a word is full of connotations of hatred, violence, injustice, and inequality. An objective definition of racism that includes much more than hateful and disrespectful thoughts or actions may very well seem extreme; however, I expect it's the little things, the "innocent" favoritism, partiality, and insensitivity that keep the races apart.

My fear is that as long as we perpetuate a subjective definition of racism, blacks will define it one way, whites another, and both groups will have license to maintain the status quo. Maybe we shouldn't let the hatred of the KKK or of militant black nationalists define what is racism. Maybe it is the most "innocuous," "innocent" forms of racism that preclude reconciliation in our country. Maybe that's the whole game Satan is playing—focus on the hatred, the violence, the injustice, and the inequality—focus on anything as long as it is a symptom and not the root cause.

Most people I know (of any race) would argue adamantly that they do not have negative thoughts or presuppositions about another race—and that any thoughts or presuppositions they might have, either positive or negative, are based on experience and therefore justified. So if a subjective definition of racism is necessary, how do we get beyond a person's individualistic justifications?

BZ

Brent,

I agree with you, it does seem somewhat odd that the white guy wants a harsher definition of racism than the black guy, but I'm not so sure I can accept such a strict definition.

Since the Tower of Babel man has had an innate bias for people who look and talk and act like he does. This is not all bad or even necessarily evil, even though this bias is sometimes a racial bias. The word "racism," at least in America, has negative connotations and implications. I would not want to water down the word by defining it with our innate bias towards those who look, act, and talk like we do. Nor would I want to cause people who are innocent of racist tendencies to feel guilty because of a very strict technical definition.

Regardless of how we define it, though, objectively or subjectively, racism still exists in America. The baffling thing to me is why many whites refuse to believe this. Are whites blind to the obvious because they would rather not see the truth? How can so many people watch the news, read a newspaper, or listen to the radio without becoming at least subconsciously aware that racism is a problem? Because of these beliefs and this blindness, reconciliation cannot happen. Until whites are ready to admit that racism still does exist (using either definition), confess that fact, and repent—our culture will be unable to heal.

How do we get beyond a person's individualistic justifications? Education, personal relational interaction (i.e., friendships), and one-on-one reconciliation.

So if education is so important, how can whites be educated about racism? I would say that other whites like you must speak up, speak out, and reach out. Of course blacks must do the same. However, as I scan the country in search of "reconcilers," I realize that one of the most important pieces to the puzzle that is missing is the presence of white voices, like Glen Kehrein and Joseph Stowell. It is when men like these, and even a man like you, speak out against racist behavior and beliefs that other whites will begin to see the truth. Let's just admit it, when a black man speaks out against racism, whites tune him out like a squeaky wheel.

The second key is personal relationships between individuals of different races. It is only within a friendship like the one we have that individuals stand a chance of reconciling racial differences.

It's only the church of Jesus Christ that has been given the ministry of reconciliation (2 Cor. 5:18–21). We Christians have failed in this mission of reconciliation so miserably that Sunday morning is the most segregated time of the week. I hope we don't continue to drop the ball.

DA

Can we ever eliminate racism and attain reconciliation?

Defining an issue such as racism is one thing. Coming to a consensus on how to remedy the issue is an entirely different matter. Just as blacks and whites often define racism differently, we also have differing ideas on what is necessary to solve the problem we face in our country. It seems that this side of heaven blacks and whites will always struggle with racism and reconciliation. Some writers and pastors these days have decided that the word *reconciliation* is the wrong word to use because our two races have never had good relations or harmony, therefore there is nothing to be reconciled back to. Do not get stuck on a Webster-like definition of *reconciliation* in a racial setting as being the *restoration* of good relations between blacks and whites. If we can simply explain and understand our differences, then we begin to have a shot at developing friendship and possibly even harmony.

David,

Your points are well made and well taken. I will confess that racism still exists in America. The question now is will we ever be able to eliminate this racism? You propose that the keys are repentance by whites, white to white education, and personal relationships between blacks and whites.

I struggle with this because rarely when there is disconnection between two people is only one person solely responsible for the lack of unity. One person can unilaterally harm a relationship, but I venture that almost all divorces occur because both parties contributed to the failure of the marriage. Maybe one party contributed significantly more than the other, but both parties contributed. Likewise, it will take both parties confessing their contribution for unity to occur.

Your statement is a common theme whites hear from blacks today. This is what I hear from this statement: "White man, you are the sole cause of our problems; you have to get right and confess your offense against me; I have done no wrong." I will admit that the white man unilaterally offended and harmed blacks with slavery and Jim Crow laws. However, I cannot concur that whites are solely responsible for the lack of unity between blacks and whites today. And I cannot concur that whites are solely responsible for all the problems blacks feel they are victimized by.

I agree that reconciliation cannot occur until whites are willing to confess and repent for offenses committed against blacks. But along the same line, reconciliation cannot occur until blacks are willing to confess and repent for their contribution to the problem too—mutual confession, not necessarily an equal amount of confession, but mutual confession.

Blacks won the fight against institutionalized racist behavior by crying out "racism," pointing out the injustice, and then bringing it before the conscience of the people who could change the laws. The fight against the racism contained within an individual's heart is an entirely different battle. However, blacks are still fighting the same way, crying "racism" and pointing a finger. This time the finger is pointed at a person instead of a law.

The battle for a person's heart and mind is not won by attacking that person; it is won by changing that person's belief system and their values. Ask the women's rights advocate. All the picketing and demonstrations in the world by prolife groups will not change that advocate's personal opinion or beliefs. Ask the evangelist who has preached vehemently about the perils of not accepting Christ as Lord and Savior—the apathetic unbeliever will not convert to Christianity, no matter how emphatic the speaker is, unless the person's heart and soul is first "moved" and "touched" by God.

Blacks can yell, scream, riot, and revolt all they want. Unless they are able to change the hearts and minds of the "racist" world, which is "oppressing" them, the battle against racism will be hopelessly lost. Every time I am accused of being racist simply because I am white, the walls go up and my accuser's words fall on deaf ears. Reconciliation will never be attained in an environment where one person (or group of persons) is accusatory and another person (or group of persons) is defensive.

Do I need to be more educated about different cultures and be made more aware of racist statements and behaviors? Sure! Do I need to seek out and build friendships with blacks other than you and the other men I work with at Bridgeway? Sure! But you know what, the most vocal people I know speaking out against us "racist" white people are black pastors. Please tell me why I should believe the sheep want to build a relationship with me, when the shepherd is publicly swinging his staff in my general direction?

BZ

Brent,

*P*lease know that I am in no way implying that whites are "solely" responsible for the disunity we now face in America. Blacks have added to the tension and strain in this tenuous relationship. However, we cannot forget the "cause and effect" relationship that has plunged us into such turmoil. It would be irresponsible to attempt to solve a fight between two schoolboys without investigating who threw the first punch and what precipitated him doing so. Likewise, it would be irrational for us to talk about reconciliation without talking about the "cause" of this turmoil.

I will admit that such a tumultuous history in no way justifies black racism against whites today. However, we can agree that an abused woman can indeed feel a sense of distrust toward the husband she is reconciling with for a period until that trust is restored, can we not?

My question to the battering husband is this: "What are you willing to do to build bridges of trust with that abused wife?" If he answers, "Well, that was a long time ago. She should just get over it so we can live in peace today," I would respond by saying, "You don't really want reconciliation. You want accommodation. You want someone to accommodate your sinful behavior so you don't have to feel the repercussions of wrong choices." If the husband truly wanted to reconcile with his wife, he would want to know what he could do to build bridges of trust again.

Brent, I heard Dr. Tony Evans once say, "We may have all come over on different ships but we're in the same boat now." I agree with this statement in that we must find a way to get along today and not focus on the past. However, God has not called you and me to simply "get along" but to commune together as brothers. The church is called to love and accept one another. Such communion goes far beyond accommodation and toleration. It is called reconciliation.

Therefore, you must ask yourself, "What must I do to build bridges of trust in order to reconcile?"

The marriage illustration is a good analogy for some of what we are discussing, however racial injustice is better compared to a criminal who invades a suburban home in the middle of the night. He ravages the property, steals the jewelry, beats the man of the house, rapes the wife, kidnaps the children, and separates them by selling them as slaves in a foreign land.

Do we expect these children from the ravaged home, or their descendants, to spend much time thinking about how to coddle the violator or his descendants in the process of reconciliation? No. What is more necessary than anything else is heartfelt repentance that rings with true sincerity. Anything less minimizes the pain that is felt.

Admittedly, blacks have sinned and messed up big time when it comes to the relations we have with whites. But first things first, whites must repent!

In one of your previous letters you stated that: "Blacks and all other minorities have achieved legal equality in America." I disagree. Maybe on the books equality exists, but when it comes to reality in the justice system, the education system, the governmental system, the media, or even in the corporate marketplace, equality remains elusive. As the prisons are overly populated by minorities and death row is lined with blacks, we must wonder if minorities are the only ones who break the law. If you were to research the number of death row sentences that are given to whites versus blacks for the same crime, you would be surprised. With a population of 14 percent in America, blacks sure populate the abundance of prisons at a much greater ratio. Blacks make less money in corporations for doing the exact same job as whites. Blacks are usually charged more money to purchase a vehicle than whites. The same is true for women. My point is that systematic and institutional racism exist. This is a problem.

You are right when you say racism is a heart problem and that yelling and screaming cannot change it. However, discrimination can be prosecuted when discovered and it can be lobbied against in all the systems I previously mentioned. But there is something very crucial we must realize; many whites don't believe that racism still exists. Many believe that it all changed with the enactment of the civil rights laws. Until such a confession exists and repentance follows, how can our culture heal?

I believe you will find that many blacks feel that a necessary component of racial reconciliation is confession and repentance. Until whites are willing to repent of the wrongs committed against blacks, reconciliation will be unattainable. How would you define racial reconciliation? Does your definition include repentance?

DA

David,

W hat do I think racial reconciliation means? Webster's primary definition of "reconciliation" is the action of restoring friendship or harmony and the action of settling or resolving diferences. I am an accountant by education and a tax accountant by profession. There is a lot of reconciling that goes on in accounting. When there is a calculated result, a number, that does not make sense (given a base of accounting theory and principles) we have to reconcile why the result was different than our expectation. In accounting there is a lot of reconciling of differences, explanations of why there was a difference, and understanding what caused the difference. Once a result has been reconciled (explained and understood), then a conclusion may be made as to whether change is needed or whether the difference is acceptable.

My friend, as we pursue racial reconciliation between us, I think we will find much explanation and much understanding of our racial differences. I think we will find that there is probably little about each other we would like the other to change. And I think we will finally understand each other more fully. I believe that our reconciliation will reveal that we are different and that it is O.K. to be different.

However, although I agree that racial reconciliation starts with and must happen first between two individuals, I think there is also a necessary macroelement. For me as a white man to say that I am racially reconciled, it will take more than reconciliation between you and me. I, like many other whites I know, can differentiate a person within a subgroup from the subgroup itself. I may be able to love you as closely as a brother, yet resent and hold things against other blacks. I think reconciliation for me (and probably many whites) will involve both the relational and macroelements. It is through these written discussions that I hope to pursue, resolve, and reconcile the macroelement.

Does racial reconciliation involve confession and repentance? If I have committed an offense towards a person or another race, then for us to be reconciled it would require that I repent of the offense. I'm not so sure however that racial reconciliation requires a confession/repentance by me for offenses committed by others.

BZ

Why are blacks so angry?

There is a growing rage in the African American community, a rage that baffles whites. Whites see examples of this simmering black rage and in a state of disbelief or shock simply shake their heads and ask, "Why are blacks so angry?" It just simply doesn't make sense to the average white person. The following letters address the issues of racial resentment, anger, and rage, within the black community but also within the white community.

David,

I attended the Indianapolis Promise Keepers rally this year and was struck by a truth I doubt I'll ever forget. Gary Smalley, a well-known speaker on marriage and how to more intimately interact in the marriage relationship, spoke on anger. His session was specifically about the anger that husbands and wives feel and the damage that unresolved anger can do to a marriage. He talked about how our anger with other people that is left unresolved for an extended period of time can affect our relationship with God and with our spouses. He stated that unresolved anger in our hearts shuts off God's work in our lives and in the life of our country. He stated that an unforgiving spirit makes it impossible to relate intimately with

God, our spouse, or with others. He even went as far as to say that angry people are unable to receive the love of God.

Toward the end of his talk Mr. Smalley offered three things that we can do to help resolve anger. One, realize that minor things for us are big deals for others. Two, humble ourselves and ask forgiveness from those we have offended. Three, humble ourselves and forgive those who have offended us. His message was potent and as he spoke, I think I began to understand why racial reconciliation is so difficult for us Americans. Blacks and whites are angry with each other.

Given the premise that unresolved anger leads to resentment and prolonged resentment leads to rage, we can then answer the question: Where did the rage of black Americans come from? Did it originate from racism experienced during the 1990s or has it festered from years of unresolved anger and racism?

My friend, I do not understand why blacks are so angry, nor why blacks have been so angry for so long that their anger has become rage. Cannot blacks see all the tremendous advances toward eliminating racial discrimination that have been made in the last thirty years? Why the hatred of whites? Slavery was a long time ago and as best as I can tell, life for blacks as a whole today is better in America than in any of the African countries their ancestors were kidnapped and enslaved from. So why so much rage? I watched in amazement the riots in South Central Los Angeles. I just do not understand how anyone could be so full of rage that they would destroy their own community. I cognizantly understand that unresolved anger is self destructive—but these riots seemed to be an extended lapse of reason, even insanity.

Why has this anger been allowed to go unresolved? Where are the pastors who are to help people understand their sins and to turn from them? Yes, it is possible to be angry and not to sin, and yes, there is such a thing as righteous anger; however, resentment and rage are not righteous, they are sin just as racism is sin. The existence of racism and discrimination does not make resentment or rage any less of a sin. Nowhere in the Scriptures did Christ or the apostles state that it is appropriate to respond to one sin with another sin; nor do the Scriptures provide that because of one sin that a different sin would no longer be considered sin.

We have this idea in America today that black rage is an appropriate, tolerable response to the racism under which blacks have been victimized. I do not believe this idea is supportable with biblical teachings. I ask again, where are the black ministers preaching to the black congregations that resentment and rage, even though natural human responses, are sin? Do these ministers exist? The majority of black ministers I see are using their position and title as a means to fuel blacks' expression of their resentment and rage—this is a travesty and a severe violation of a minister's fiduciary duty of "shepherding the flock." God holds spiritual leaders accountable for the teaching and guidance they provide. I pity the minister that must answer to God for stirring up the emotions of resentment and rage within His people.

BZ

Brent,

*Y*ou asked, "Cannot blacks see all the tremendous advances toward eliminating racial discrimination that have been made in the last thirty years? Why the hatred of whites? Slavery was a long time ago and as best as I can tell, life for blacks as a whole today is better in America than in any of the African countries their ancestors were kidnapped from. Why so much rage?"

Boy, are these loaded statements. When a girl is kidnapped and raped, should the criminal expect the father of the girl, or even the actual victim, to have gratitude toward him for releasing her? Just because blacks are no longer enslaved doesn't mean that the anger or the effects of the crime simply dissipate. What is a black man supposed to say? Thank you? The kidnap and rape victim will naturally be angry if she lives in a world where kidnappings and rapes continue to occur. In fact she may start an organization or a movement that would battle against such behavior. If this organization grows and continues to grow for generations to come, then there would always be a keen awareness against kidnappers. There may even be support groups for those who are present-day victims. At any rate, the reality of such crimes is kept alive. However, the danger is that these rape victims would indict all men and be suspicious of all men because of their cause.

This same danger and tension exist in the black community. While struggling against the injustices of racism and discrimination, it's real easy to condemn, indict, and be suspicious of all whites.

Blacks have had to fight for every inch of freedom, respect, and privilege that has been gained. The feeling and mentality are that no one has given us anything. So when you say we're moving forward and advancing, it's not as if blacks are somehow feeling thankful to whites for it. There is still no remorse or repentance from the white-led government. The black man is saying, "In order for me to succeed, I have to be twice as smart, twice as qualified, and twice as lucky to be competitive with the white man. No one is going to help me but myself." This is the attitude of your educated, middle- and upper-class black person who has succeeded in government or corporate America.

So what are blacks to do who are frustrated with their status personally or with the status of their people? If we band together, pool our resources, have rallies to promote racial unity—whites get scared. If we stay separate, we risk losing an important power and political base.

We need leadership that is nonthreatening to whites and noncompromising for blacks. It's a tightrope to walk.

The responsibility of blacks is to forgive and move on. Of course that is easier said than done. Especially when you live in a system that is still bent towards discrimination. Black preachers and other community leaders haven't helped this process. You stated in your letter your distaste and anger towards the black leadership, especially preachers. You are absolutely right—and these men will be held accountable for teaching "hard-heartedness" instead of forgiveness. They have fallen into the same trap as the rape victim. It's the "condemn all" trap.

All of us are susceptible to falling into such a "perfectly engineered" trap. Satan's job is to trap us in our own hatred and selfishness. Jesus' job is to set us free so we can express selflessness.

Your observation about anger and racial reconciliation is correct. Whites and blacks are angry with each other. I'm curious, though, what your take on the other side of the coin is? We've talked about black rage; what about the anger of whites? How is this affecting reconciliation?

DA

David,

I learned two things from Gary Smalley. The first we've talked about; the second was about myself. For the first time I realized that I have been harboring anger in my heart. Anger that has gone unresolved long enough that it has grown into resentment, a resentment that is racially based, a resentment against blacks collectively, but not against blacks individually. I do not resent you, my friend, nor do I resent the accounting clerk in my office nor the friend I had in college from the inner city of Indiana nor do I resent the stranger I pass on the street. This leads me to believe that my frustration, anger, and resentment are founded on something other than my being a racist. I would expect a racist to dislike both the individual and the individual's racial group. I believe that my feelings are toward the responses and actions of a group of people rather than toward the genetics (i.e., being black) of the group. Nevertheless, although I do not believe my anger and resentment to be racist, it is still sin and therefore it is my responsibility to confess this sin and then to not commit this sin again.

I do not think I fully understand yet the depth of my resentful feelings but I anticipate that as we correspond, the focal points will become obvious. There is one thing I am not so sure I know how to do, though—how to stop being angry.

You asked about white anger. I would guess that I am not alone, that I am not the only white man with racial resentment or anger in his heart. How does this affect reconciliation? In friendships and marriages it is only when both parties value the relationship that an offense may be reconciled. Blacks are very, very angry at whites over past and present racial injustices. Whites are angry at blacks because so much has been done to change the sins of the past yet blacks are still very, very angry. Whites and blacks typically don't live in the same neighborhood, go to the same churches, or go to the same schools. Without the basic interactions in those areas, how can we value relationships with each other? If a relationship has no value, then who cares if there's reconciliation or not, it's not a priority.

BZ

Brent,

*R*egarding your anger, thank you for confessing your feelings honestly. I realize that it is easy to be angry or even resentful toward a group for the pain or problems that a representative of that group may have caused. However, the sentiments you are expressing are the exact same ones that blacks express regarding whites. There are blacks who are angry and resentful toward whites although there may be one or two or three whites whom they would deem as "cool" or "okay."

Your feelings are normal and natural, but ungodly. I know that you realize this or you would not have said in your last correspondence, "Although I do not believe my anger and resentment to be racist, it is still sin and therefore it is my responsibility to confess this sin and then to not commit this sin again."

I wholeheartedly agree with the fact that anger can lead to sin and in your case, you may be sinning by harboring resentment in your heart. Your confession is healthy and honest and is the first step to healing. However, I disagree with the first part of your statement that I just quoted. Believe me, brother, your feelings of negativity and resentment are a hotbed where racism is being nurtured.

You must resist the temptation of lumping all blacks together when it comes to your anger. By saying to me that you have "resentment against blacks collectively, but not against blacks individually" is like my saying to you, I have resentment toward accountants, but not you.

Although, there is a compliment in there somewhere, the bottom line is that I have a prejudice against accountants in general and you are an exception. Your words have revealed that you have a prejudice against blacks in general and I am an exception.

How do you get out of this prejudicial pattern? First, confess the sin of racism to God and ask Him to give you the grace to see people as image-bearers of Him. Secondly, befriend and begin relating to more blacks to offset your obvious imbalance. This has to be intentional because it won't happen naturally. Like evangelism, we must be intentional about it.

I openly admit that blacks have a lot of problems as all people do. But we must assess people as individuals with distinctions. All Jews are not money-grabbers. All Asians are not inner-city business predators. All Hispanics are not thieves. All blacks are not lazy, and all whites are not mass-murderers or self-absorbed. All these groups are of one race, the human race. They all bear God's image and that is where we must begin. This is the mindset that offsets the racist mentality.

The minute I allow my mind and heart to accept these stereotypes as truths regarding an entire group, I have become a born-again racist.

Of course I understand that all groups have certain distinctions that are noticeable, possibly negative, and sometimes even admirable, but we must be careful in how we permit ourselves to think.

Reconciliation takes effort, my brother,* the same kind of effort these letters take. It will cost you something if you truly want to be a reconciler because it means that you might have to move your home or purposely sit next to that person who is different than you on the train to get to know them. We are all a part of one race, the human race. Mankind is sinful and I have no doubt that people of my skin tone live out sinful behaviors daily. So do yours. If I were to base my opinion of whites on my negative experiences, I would never be a reconciler. I base my view of people in general on the fact that the awesome God of creation creates them and that it is His image they bear.

A great place to start in dealing with your anger is confession and repentance before the Lord for your sin, and then build relationships with others by intentional effort.

In another but similar vein, I really appreciated the attached article regarding peacemakers in Moody magazine.** This is what we must become. Please give me your comments regarding this editorial when you have time.

DA

David,

I take your observations and counsel to heart and understand that it is these very prejudices that make my own personal racial reconciliation so necessary. I certainly do not desire to intentionally

---

*Specific efforts that can be made in reconciliation are provided in appendix A.

**See this article reprinted in appendix B.

or inadvertently nurture racism and hopefully I'm a step or two closer to rooting out the "hotbed" within me.

Before I go on to the article out of Moody I want to ask a clarifying question or two because I'm feeling a little beat up. Is it possible to have a prejudice against or resentment towards people of another race without being labeled racist? If a person's prejudice, resentment, or anger is the result of inappropriate behavior on the part of members of the other race, does the inappropriate behavior exempt the resulting prejudice or anger from being considered "racist"?

My confession wasn't so much that "I'm a racist, please forgive me" as it was "I have been harboring resentment in my heart towards blacks, please forgive me." If my resentment is without merit, meaning not the result of an inappropriate behavior observed or experienced, then it seems clear that it would be racism. But if any prejudice, resentment, or anger, regardless of legitimacy or illegitimacy, is racist, then I don't feel so bad about being beat up because almost every person in the world is guilty along with me. If my resentment can be considered racism, if the anger of white supremacists can be considered racist, then cannot the continuing anger of blacks over slavery and segregation also be considered racist? Cannot even the resentment of blacks about today's perceived inequalities and injustices also be considered racist?

Whether my resentment is with or without justification, whether it is racist or not—it is still sin and an ungodly attitude. So tell me, are we all guilty? Or just us white guys?

BZ

Brent,

Blacks are as guilty as whites when it comes to being racist. In my opinion, anyone who harbors negative attitudes towards someone else based on their color or culture is a racist. Harboring anger and resentment is sin, period. Attitudes and actions that cause one to believe and behave negatively due to stored up anger is sin. We both know that racism is not a skin problem, but a sin problem.

Regarding the issue of labels, a "racist" is not someone who has a racist thought or commits a single act. A "racist" is someone with a condition and/or predisposition to act or think negatively towards someone else due to a race-based mentality.

Brent, you and I may or may not be racists. We can only know this through self-examination. The following questions may help us in our self-analysis:

1. What is my mentality and attitude toward those who are different than me?
2. What conversations do I participate in regarding other people groups?
3. What actions do I commit that are based on my mentality regarding other people?*

DA

---

*See questions in appendix A for your own self-analysis.

Is another civil war coming?

This question may have caught you by surprise and you wonder, Why would there be another civil war? The real issue here is that of ethnic violence and what we as Christians are doing to be the peacemakers we have been instructed to be. The thought of inner-city "ethnic" violence coming into suburban or rural backyards terrifies many whites, and the continuing escalation of incidents of violence by groups of one or another racial persuasion undeniably shape our perceptions of each other. The question simply asks: How close are we to a widespread outbreak of racially motivated violence?

David,

*I*n response to your request, I will comment on the June 1994 editorial out of Moody magazine entitled "Blessed Are the Peacemakers."*

The editor makes an interesting comment regarding ethnic hatred and violence in Somalia, Sudan, Bosnia, and Rwanda when he states "For years these people have been sowing seeds of mistrust, hatred, and injustice. Now they are reaping what they have sown." After reading this article two questions immediately come to mind. When does America reap what has been sown? When do the years of mis-

*See appendix B.

40

trust, hatred, and injustice in America explode into ethnic violence?

We like to think the violence of Bosnia and Rwanda could never happen in the United States, that we are permanently insulated from the tragedy by thousands of miles over deep oceans. We like to think we are more civilized than the former Yugoslavians or a third world country. In all likelihood we never will experience such tragedies in our own backyard, but there are no guarantees as the storm warnings of escalating racial tensions and the deepening rage of black Americans grow more foreboding. We like to think the problems are contained in the big cities, that suburbia and rural America are immune to the conflicts. But are they? The theory that exists and the implication in the editorial is that without racial reconciliation on a grand scale, the United States could itself experience ethnic violence extensive enough to be considered a civil war.

I have a difficult time believing the theory that says America is approaching another civil war; however, it is hard to deny that the propensity toward ethnic violence in America is increasing each year. This leads me to ask, Where are the peacemakers? How come there are so few peacemakers, either white or black? Lastly, how can we reverse the trend and be peacemakers and attain racial reconciliation?

BZ

Brent,

*D*ue to a shortage of time today I'm going to respond to your last letter in two parts. I'll take the short response today.

You asked: Where are the peacemakers? And why are there so few peacemakers?

These are great questions. I truly believe that God has called you and me to be peacemakers, along with all other Christians. The problem is that historically Christians have been remiss when it comes to taking leadership in making peace. We seem to have confused peacemaking with peacekeeping and have remained inactive or reactive to the very things God tells us to be proactive about. He tells us to be proactive in our dealings with the poor and hurting (Matt. 25:45). He tells us to reflect His character with regard to justice and righteousness and kindness (Jer. 9:24). He even tells us to stand against racism and build bridges in His name (Gal. 2:14). But unfortunately we wait around for the "evangelically correct" bandwagon to come rolling around before we jump out to make a difference!

It is important to notice something about the Son of God's example. Jesus Himself was proactive in bringing salvation to us. He was proactive in crossing spiritual, social, economical, and racial lines for the sake of the gospel. Because of God's proactive nature, you and I are saved from sin's eternal trap.

Jesus was proactive in making peace with you and me, even though we did not desire peace with Him (Eph. 2:1–9). Thus we were reactive to His proactivity.

My point is that Christians should not be on the reactive side of making a difference for Christ. If we are to follow His divine example, then we must be proactive in evangelism, justice, kindness, mercy, and the like.* Although this may mean different things for different Christians, it sure does not mean ignore the issue!

Maybe this is why Jesus' statement about peacemakers is the only one that mentions being called "sons of God" (Matt. 5:9). Maybe Jesus knew that proactive peacemakers

*Examples of proactive measures are service in the inner city, short-term mission trips, involvement in the lives of "at risk" teens, and service to the hurting and elderly. Christians can be on the forefront of making a difference in the area of politics, social services, or work in the legal system. Also Christians can be so much more proactive than we have been in the past in teaching our children about race relations and racism. Christian parents can model reconciliation to their children by interacting with an array of multicultural friends.

who address issues, such as racism, were somehow worthy to be called "sons of God."

DA

Brent,

Continuing in response to your comments on the editorial "Blessed Are the Peacemakers." In your letter you asked, "When does America reap what has been sown?" and "When do the years of mistrust, hatred, and injustice in America explode into ethnic violence?"

I believe that right now America is reaping what has been sown. All of the anger, bitterness, media hype, and rage is a present demonstration of past and present criminal offenses against the African American people.

While none of us can go back and change the past, I believe that before we can focus on the future we must first deal with the past and the present, honestly and accurately. America has never truly repented of her racial misconduct. You will hear white voices say that slavery was wrong and that it was a "terrible thing." But yet it will not be taught properly in the history books; nor will African American history be taught as a required course. As a result, blacks grow up with no real knowledge and understanding of who they are, how they were represented, nor of the contribution they made to the development of this great country. The educational wing of our society refuses to tell the truth about slavery, black heroes, and the foundational shoulders on which this great country has been built other than just George Washington, Abe Lincoln, etc.

Because of this noncooperation by a white-led government, blacks have been forced to start organizations, periodicals, and separatist groups to inform ourselves and look out for our own interests. If we don't, who will? Civil rights organizations like the NAACP, National Black Caucus, and, yes, even the Nation of Islam, etc. have been formed to help blacks struggle for every inch of freedom and equality that has been won (i.e., voting rights, desegregated schools, laws against discriminatory hiring practices, etc.).

So guess what happens? The eighteen-to-twenty-year-old African American decides that he wants to know about his history and his roots. Where does he go? If he goes to college, specifically an all-black college, he will learn how he fits into history. He then becomes angry because he was never told nor taught as a youngster in the public school system about his roots in America (whites are taught about their history). Then he looks around at the lingering effects of slavery and discrimination (i.e., project housing, low self-image, broken homes, drugs, lack of opportunity to achieve the American dream, etc.) and says to himself, "Aha, that's why things are the way they are. I'm ticked!"

Couple this new learning with the old experiences that his fifty-year-old parents and/or his seventy-five-year-old grandmother have told him about while growing up and we can see why he is angry. Notice that this fictitious person is a college student who will one day be in corporate America, joining the black middle class. This may explain the anger of the black middle class that has been gaining so much press lately.

The white media will ask, "Why would the black middle class be angry when things are so much better for them?" Just because they have an education and a paycheck doesn't change the fact that they are black. They still feel the pain associated with their culture. There are some things money and education cannot take away. Only a forgiving heart given by a grace-giving God can heal such pain.

Finally, if this is the pain an educated, moneymaking black man feels, can you imagine how a poverty-stricken, gang-surviving, hopeless-hearted black man would feel?*

Brent, please understand that this explanation is just that, an explanation. I believe that these are some of the key reasons why we see the anger that has infected the African

---

*The black middle class is growing rapidly in America. Those blacks at poverty levels will often feel an even greater sense of despair and, often, anger because of their powerlessness.

American community. This is in no way an excuse for behavior of violence or racial enmity. It is an explanation. I do not excuse racism in any form, no more than I would excuse the killing of an abortion doctor to stop abortions. Even though it's possible to explain such a heinous crime, we cannot excuse nor condone it!

Finally, in answer to your second question about the timing of the ethnic explosion, I do not know. I hope never! However, as I look around the world at all the racial and ethnic violence I'm not sure what makes America any different. Our moral capacity is no better than anyone else's. We are just as capable of a civil war as other countries. We have done it before. We can do it again.

This is why it is so incredibly important that the true cause of Christ is forwarded. He did not call His disciples to save people and then die. He called His disciples to love God, love one another, and be a light. This was a multicultural command that Jesus Himself modeled. This dynamic sharing, caring, and load bearing was unprecedented before Jesus' ministry on earth.

So then, will we follow Jesus' example or will the black church cover their eyes and say, "Oh my, we live in such an unjust and unequal world. Oh well, we're just pilgrims." Will the white church continue to teach expositional passages and forsake the meaning of those passages by saying, "Oh my, we live in such a mean and angry world. Oh well, we're just pilgrims."

May it never be! May we be the generation of Christians that model the first-century church and follow the lead of our Lord by being peacemakers!*

DA

---

*The first-century church was inaugurated in Acts 2. This gathering in the streets of Jerusalem was a multicultural gathering of people representing different languages and cultural groups. After this inauguration of the church, we find a multicultural community of believers growing and thriving as they prevailed in fulfilling the great command and the Great Commission.

Brent,

*I*n my study time today I reread our last few letters on anger and ethnic violence and wanted to say a few more things about this theory of a second American civil war.

You stated your disbelief that America could be approaching another civil war, a race war. Remember, though, if it is possible to fight other people's battles (Kuwait, Haiti, Somalia, etc.), it is sure possible for us to fight one another.

However, I do not fear a civil war between races in our country, not because such a thought wouldn't scare me, but because I know that things are going to get worse and I'm prepared for expressions of evil to play themselves out in this sinful generation. This is to be expected in the last days. It's within the doors of the church where the difference must be made. I continually come back to this point because it is central to our discussions. Sin is rampant. Racism and domination are natural. Anger and rage are human. We will never get away from this until heaven. To think otherwise is to have a utopian mentality unrooted in Scripture.

If the battle wasn't between blacks and whites, it would be between Asians and Europeans, or Indians and Hispanics, etc. It really has little to do with the issue of race. It has everything to do with pride, arrogance, domination, and forgiveness. It's all about power and subjection. This evil isn't inherent in any particular culture or race. It's innate in natural man.

Even given this premise, we must understand that many blacks view the white man as evil, conniving, and unworthy of trust. In the minds of many blacks, the history of the white man in America proves it. Many Asians feel the same way, as do many Native Americans. Of course, I'm sure we could list how whites feel about the groups I just mentioned as well. The point is this: Only relationships can break down the barrier of stereotypes and only the love of Christ can break down the history of hatred and distrust.

The bottom line is this: You and I must guard our hearts from being pulled in by our own fleshly desire to believe that any group of people are violent, evil, or untrustworthy. This is just not true. All men and women have the same depraved capacity for evil. Only Christ can bring hope in this regard.

DA

Why is everything a racial issue with blacks?

Whites may be totally confused by black rage, but the question that leaves most whites frustrated and exasperated is this question of why everything is a racial issue with blacks. Injustice, the race card, and O. J. Simpson—to have any serious discussion on racial matters in the United States, you have to enter onto the thin ice of these topics. As desirable as it may be to avoid this difficult and polarizing conversation—you simply have to work through the differences. There is no greater example in recent memory of the vastly differing perspective blacks and whites have on matters involving our justice system than the O. J. Simpson case. The O. J. criminal trial is now a permanent moment in history. From the day Nicole Brown Simpson and Ron Goldman were murdered, there could no longer be a complete discussion of racial matters in our country without a discussion of the O. J. case and the polarized perspectives our races held as to the only logical explanation of the events that occurred. Before you read our opinions, what is yours? Are African Americans imagining discrimination in the justice system and other U.S. institutions or are whites oblivious to reality?

David,

*I*n one of your initial letters you stated that we live in a world system that is not fair. I agree. Remember when as a kid you would plead with your mother, "But it's not fair," what would she say in response? "Nobody ever said life was fair." Unfortunate as it may be, we live in a world full of injustice, daily injustice. You stated in your letter that this unfair world system needs to be changed, and I guess I agree with that, I just wonder if change is possible.

The founding fathers of this country dreamed of and tried to create a country where the common man could obtain justice, a country where all citizens whether rich or poor were given an equal opportunity for justice. On the whole and over time I would say this country has done fairly well at achieving this goal. I would say it has not been a painless process, but today we have a country that people from all over the world emulate and want to immigrate to. People come to America for freedom whether it is religious freedom or just the freedom to be the best they can be and to achieve the "American dream." In comparison to some parts of the world, life is pretty good here and I would rather have our problems than any other country's problems.

I'm sure you would agree that one of the most significant injustices in our country (past more than present) is racism. But even though racism is an injustice experienced by many minorities, not all injustices experienced are caused by racism. Sometimes an injustice is racism, and sometimes an injustice is merely that—an injustice.

Racism is an injustice that should be eliminated or at least limited if it cannot be eliminated. What I do not understand, though, is why it appears that blacks believe that every injustice they experience is the result of racism? And along the same line, why is it that every action that is not perceived to be positive for blacks is branded racism? Why is everything a racial issue? It seems like a crutch or a universal excuse to pass responsibility on to someone else. The belief that all injustices experienced by blacks are either direct racism or the indirect result of racism is exasperating to whites and probably one of the largest reasons whites on a personal level try to keep blacks at a distance.

The little boy in the children's story cried "wolf" too many times, so many that when the wolf was really there, no one cared or believed him. I sense that the black community is headed on the course to where they will have cried "racism" so many times when the rest of the world has not seen racism that eventually a genuine victim of racism will cry out "racism"—and no one will care. The axiom holds true for blacks too—choose your battles wisely. Crying "racism" every time an injustice is experienced or on every occasion that is not perceived as being completely positive for blacks as a whole does not elicit compassion nor does it motivate heart change in whites. I do not know how others feel but I am tired of the complaining, the excuses, and the finger-pointing.

BZ

Brent,

I agree. There is a lot of "wolf crying" out there with regard to racism. This is unfortunate, and I believe a hindrance to the cause of eliminating racist beliefs and behavior in our country. To be honest I wish more black leaders would crack down on such hypocrisy and that fewer would play the race card.

As to why everything is a racial issue for blacks. I believe it is simply because, whether we like it or not, everything is a race issue today. It's not going to get any better either. America has created a terrible animal that is growing into a vicious creature. This creature called racism will not easily be slain. We are reaping what we have sown, and our American history is now our present problem.

It's not enough to tell blacks to "get over it" or "stop making such a big issue out of race." Race has been the issue since blacks got off the slave ships. For whites to tell blacks to forget about race and become one with the majority race isn't practical nor is it sensitive. Blacks as a people are very self-conscious about their race.

50

The only way for America to win the race war is to have a higher common denominator that would unify all Americans. I don't know what that denominator is for the world; however, for Christians, it's Christ. We as Christians must identify with our new race in Christ Jesus. He is our greatest unifying denominator.

DA

David,

I want to thank you for the acknowledgment that in the black community there is a fair amount of "crying wolf" about racism. It is good to hear a black pastor say that playing the "race card" should be stopped. It gives me hope that whites and blacks can see eye to eye and that blacks and whites together can discern true racism.

I do want to go back to my question, "Why is everything a racial issue with blacks?" I've read your response and to be honest I'm still confused and I still don't understand.

You said that "blacks as a people are very self-conscious about their race." I would add that Jewish people are also very self-conscious about their race.

I've been friends with several Jewish people in my life. Yes, they are very sensitive about the Holocaust, Nazism, and neo-Nazism. Yes, they support the dogmatic pursuit of Nazi war criminals that are still at large. But I've never gotten the sense that there remains a festering hatred of all Germans. I've never gotten the sense that everything is an anti-Semitism issue.

So please, help me understand why is everything a racial issue with blacks?

BZ

Brent,

*R*egarding this question of "Why is everything a racial issue with blacks?" I stand by my original answer that blacks have been made very conscious about their race, and thus we have become a self-conscious people. When someone has a handicap, it is easy to say, "Don't be self-conscious about your handicap," but in all reality it takes a mountain-full of self-esteem to live with a handicap or some other undesirable feature that is noticeable to all. (Black skin was undesirable for a long time and in some cases still is.)

Regarding Jewish people, everything may not be a race issue, but they are very sensitive about their culture. First, Jewish history of persecution goes back to Germany not America. Although there are issues of anti-Semitism in America, Jews have gotten their respect. Many have money, power, and education. However, the Jews who live in Germany would be a better parallel to blacks in America. Otherwise, we are comparing apples to oranges. Another way of looking at it is thinking of blacks migrating to Europe. There is not the same history there as there is here in America; therefore blacks in Europe would deal with racial issues differently. Blacks in Europe would be a better parallel with Jews in America, and Jews in Germany would be a closer parallel with blacks in America. But the black man's history of persecution is primarily here in America. That's the difference.

In addition, Jews have gotten the respect of Americans. All people have shunned the Holocaust. There are museums, movies, and outcry from religious leaders regarding the Nazi oppression. But do Jews get the same respect in the country where their oppression took place? Do blacks get it in America? There have been no National Days of Repentance, no museums, or admission of guilt. And by the way, ending slavery is as much an admission of guilt as is a man's ending his violent assault of rape. Stopping the violent act is one thing; repentance, repayment when possible, and reconciliation is something else.

Secondly, about the Jews in whom you don't sense strong sensitivity about their Jewishness: Many Jews do not have distinguishable ethnic features and therefore they don't receive the same volume of discrimination nor are they made to feel as self-conscious as blacks. The only parallel I can think of is wearing a yarmulke. If a Jewish person were to wear a yarmulke to the business office every day, he would stand out. This would be the closest parallel to being black that I know of. Many times a Jewish person forgets it's on his head until someone else brings it up or until he's treated differently. This explains the self-consciousness of many blacks. They are easily distinguishable but they can't remove their skin like a yarmulke.

If you would like to experience the feeling of being a minority, wear a yarmulke for a week, on the trains, in restaurants, to gas stations, etc. The best parallel would be for you to do this in Germany! Do you get my drift? I think you would be self-conscious too. It would take a whole lot more than telling you, "Don't be self-conscious" for you to get over your feelings of standing out and being judged. It's a lot to ask someone, "Don't think about your handicap, your distinguishable feature, your yarmulke, your race." Easier said than done, right?

DA

David,

O.K. I hear what you're saying, but the day-to-day examples of what appear to me to be classic cases of playing the race card are completely exasperating. Let's talk about O. J.

Attached is an article by Clarence Page, a Chicago Tribune columnist, discussing a CNN-USA Today poll about the O. J. Simpson case.* Allegations are being made by blacks that the case is receiving unusually large amounts of media coverage because a black man has been charged with the murders of his white wife and white male friend. The poll reveals that the majority of blacks believe O. J. Simpson to be the victim of racism.

*See the article in appendix B

Reading this article I was at a loss to understand how the majority of blacks could be so obsessed with and paranoid of racism that this particular case, the double murders of Nicole Brown Simpson and Ronald Goldman, could be viewed as white racism. The allegation being made by blacks states that if O. J. were charged with murders of a black wife and her black friend that the nation would not care. This is absolutely preposterous.

From a television ratings standpoint only the Persian Gulf War was watched by more households than the police pursuit of O. J. Simpson and Al Cowlings down a nearly abandoned Los Angeles expressway at speeds far below the speed limit. Not only did millions of households watch the pursuit on television but almost every car on that expressway had pulled off to the side and stopped to watch the parade of the white Bronco with police trailing behind.

Mr. Page and many other blacks want us to believe this is simply a case of black man killing white woman and white man. This would be an unprecedented simultaneous display of malicious racism accompanied by a lynch mob mentality by millions of people across not only the nation but also the globe. Mr. Page's theory dehumanizes O. J. in the most significant way and fails to account for significant factors of this case that have made it so enticing to the entire nation. Never before has so public a figure been charged in such a heinous crime. O. J. Simpson's name is as recognized in this country as the names of Michael Jordan, Magic Johnson, Bill Clinton, and Ronald Reagan. O. J. was different though. He was not just a hall of fame sports hero, he was a successful sports commentator and a longtime endorsement man for Hertz rental cars. O. J. was not just successful in one aspect of life, he was successful in many, and his successes were displayed on network television over two decades.

The excitement surrounding this case not only comes from the lure of a hero falling from grace but is partly driven by the hero's fugitive status and public flight from the law. It is a murder mystery story played out everyday on our television screens. Did O. J. do it? Or is he innocent? Every person in America watching television or reading a newspaper or magazine gets to be the detective, gets to view the evidence, and gets to determine day by day who-done-it. Never before has America been presented with such an opportunity, a real-life opportunity, not just a made-for-television story.

The O. J. Simpson case is many things all at once. This is not about racism; it is about sensationalism. Blacks' charges of racism in this case are a pathetic obsession with and paranoia of sins of the past and a futile attempt to deny that a rags-to-riches hero may have actually committed two brutal murders. Innocent or guilty, racism is not an issue in this case.

I am beginning to ask myself not only the question, Why is everything a racial issue with blacks? but also, Does the black community possess the ability anymore to rightly discern what truly is racism rather than mere injustice, misfortune, embarrassment, or criminal behavior? Or is it that the black community is able to rightly discern racism vs. injustice; they just prefer to play the "race card" and blanketly call all injustice racism?

BZ

———————

Brent,

*R*egarding the O. J. trial and the Clarence Page article, boy . . . what can I say? It is laced with race, fame, money, and so many divisive issues, I'm not sure if this can qualify as a reasonable example to discuss. What I mean by this is that the O. J. trial is an opportunity for every special-interest group from the media, to battered wives, to blacks, to sports advocates to springboard their cause. I don't think Clarence Page is any different.

What he is bringing to light and what most blacks are trying to bring to light in this matter is the injustice that blacks have suffered through the years until this day. Coming to light is the enormous gulf between blacks who do not trust the legal system and whites who do trust the legal system. This popular trial is a springboard issue for many groups and I don't think you can judge what black Americans really believe about O. J. in this matter. For many blacks, it is not about O. J., really. Most blacks know that you cannot live in this country without race being an issue and you certainly cannot go to trial without it being an issue. The question must be: "To what degree is race an issue?"

DA

Equality in what and for whom?

Equal opportunity, a level playing field, true equality—these are the battle cries of blacks today. No one disputes that for centuries blacks were treated as second-class humans by whites. But equality and equal opportunity are not tangibles; they are intangible and it is almost impossible to quantify when they have been achieved. Slavery was a tangible that could be dealt with. Equality is an elusive intangible.

As with most issues that have racial implications, this topic is polarizing, emotional, and almost impossible to discuss face-to-face without raised voices and hard feelings. People on both sides of this discussion easily begin to feel marginalized. Almost every one of us could point out instances in our lives where we felt that we were victims of inequality. In the following discussion Brent raises an instance in his career where he felt his compensation was inequitable. Although most of us have felt the sting of inequality at one time or another, we still struggle because of the tendency towards an inverse relationship between overcoming inequality and compassion toward those who are still facing inequality. If we feel that we made a significant contribution in overcoming the inequality we faced, we may be less compassionate toward those still pursuing equality. But regardless of whether we have achieved our desired equality or if it remains an elusive goal—the issue remains a cold war with both sides ready to do battle.

David,

*I*n one of your previous letters you touched on the issue of equality and equal opportunity and stated that both remain elusive for minorities. Your letter stated that even though the laws say all people are equal, there is effectively no legal equality in this country. You state that the justice system, the education system, the governmental system, the media, and the corporate marketplace are discriminatory and not all people are treated the same or get to play by the same rules. The contextual implication is that blacks are discriminated against in those systems by whites because of the racism of those whites. I agree that the systems are discriminatory and inequitable; I disagree that the inequity is exclusively racially motivated. Why? Because I'm discriminated against by those same systems too.

If I had been arrested and charged with the crimes O. J. Simpson has, I probably would have been convicted by now. O. J. received preferential treatment by the justice system because O. J. could afford the best defense lawyers money could buy. I could hire an attorney, but my money would run out quickly, even if they had a low billing rate. On the books, O. J. and I would have legal equality. Effectively I am being discriminated against because of my lack of money.

My college education is from a small Southern Baptist University in Missouri; if I had been able to go to Harvard, I'd be making more money by now. My education is generally perceived to be of less quality than a Harvard education. Again a lack of money has forced me to play on a different playing field than those who were able to attend an Ivy League school.

If my wife and I continue to live in Mokena, Illinois, our children will get a good education, not as good as if we lived in the north suburbs, but we couldn't afford the housing or the taxes there.

In my job I perform the same responsibilities as the person I sit next to, except I handle more research and technical matters. I have a master's degree; my coworker doesn't.

We both have the same number of years of experience and neither one of us performs our jobs drastically better than the other. Yet if my information is correct, my coworker earns $2,000 per year in salary more than I do.

My point is this: Inequality is a fact of life and no respecter of races. Legal equality "on the books" may be the best equality that is ever achieved, not just for blacks but also for all races and both genders. I agree in theory that all people should be equally treated and have the same opportunities as all other peoples. The problem is whose "equality" is the standard? If blacks want to be treated the same as whites, you then have to ask the question, which whites? poor whites? middle-class whites? wealthy whites?

Discrimination and inequity based on economic class status is innate in a capitalistic society. The only way to create economic equity is to implement a communistic system. I believe we have more than enough real-life examples of countries that have tried communism and learned that all they achieved was equity at a poverty level. Everybody was poor and miserable except for a few controlling elite.

If the standard blacks wish to achieve is equity with middle-class whites, I think they will be disappointed to find that even when they attain this middle-class equity, there will continue to be inequity. To say that the lack of economic "equity" or that the side effects of economic inequity are racist appears to me to be smothered in self-pity and playing upon emotional issues that are not the root cause of the issue. So what is the "equity" that blacks seek? Is it intangible or tangible? Is it even attainable in a raceless environment?

BZ

Brent,

*I*f I could summarize your last letter in one sentence, it would be: Inequality and discrimination are facts of life for everyone, so stop whining, black man.

Let me ask you this question, Brent: If I had a three-year-old child and I placed that child in the middle of the inner city and said to him, "Life is unfair, son—deal with it," and then drove off, what kind of father would I be? If a blind person needed a ride and I said to that person, "Life has dealt all of us a bad hand. Here are the keys to the car. Now drive!" what kind of Christian would I be?

Fairness and inequality really aren't the crux of the problem, Brent. Sensitivity, compassion, and justice are the true issues. The Bible says, "He has showed you, O man, what is good. And what does the Lord require of you? To act justly and to love mercy and to walk humbly with your God" (Micah 6:8 NIV).

The issue of justice can never be brought down to the lowest level of saying, "Because I experience pain, you should too." If Christ took that view having suffered on the cross, where would we be today?

I will admit to you that there is a great tension between two extremes: blacks who whine and whites who oppress, but somewhere in the middle there is room for dialogue about equality and justice. To say that there will always be some inequality at some levels is accurate. For instance, the examples you gave about your workplace, salary structure, your education, etc. However, we must note that inequality based on personhood is different than inequality based on economics and education.

When a black man is denied access to a job because of his skin color, he is discriminated against in an area where he can never change. You can always get a raise. Your child can always get a better education. A black man will always be black. A woman will always be a woman.

I do not believe that minorities ought to use their status to whine, cry, or have a victim's mentality. However, for a man to punch another man in the face and then say, "Stop whining; that doesn't hurt; I have pain too," is cruel.

If two men are running a race but one has a ball and chain on his ankle, is that a fair race? Of course not. Now imagine the constrained man being freed from the hindrance of the ball and chain after running a mile or two. Is the race fair yet? No! Why? Because the unrestricted runner is way ahead due to the ball and chain that was on his opponent's ankle. The only way this race becomes fair is if the two runners start over, right?*

My point is this: As a white man, you cannot compare yourself with the other whites ("freed" runners, if you will) to measure inequality. The comparison between you and another white man in your office who is making $2,000 more than you is like you comparing yourself to other freed runners in a race. If you want a true comparison of equality versus inequality, you must compare yourself to the runner who started the race with the ball and chain on. This is the disparity between blacks and whites. This is the real distance in equality between blacks and whites.

The question isn't, Are you making a couple thousand more or less than your white colleague? The question is, How many black colleagues are even in your company to compare salaries with? How about in management? This is the real question. This is the disparity.

Blacks aren't looking for equality with whites per se. Blacks are looking for justice, fairness, and the same equal access as whites. Blacks are looking for a level playing field.**

DA

David,

*Y*our summary sentence didn't go far enough. I would summarize the opinion in my last letter as, Certain forms of inequality and discrimination

*Of course it is impossible to turn back the clock and start over. Therefore whites and blacks must focus on reconciliation with good faith efforts. Whites must aim for equal access and the sharing of power. Blacks must aim for forgiveness and moving on. Blacks must also take advantage of the many opportunities that are currently available for minorities.

**Justice means fairness in the access of opportunity and the condemnation of exploitation, inequality, and discrimination when discovered.

are in reality a fact of life for everyone. Quit whining and deal with it. I don't care who the whiner is, a man or woman, black or white—whining achieves nothing. The question in my letter was genuine. People of all races, genders, social classes, etc. want equality. But at what level do you measure equality?

You asked, "How many black colleagues are even in your company to compare salaries with? How about in management?" Throughout my career I have only known two blacks that were employed in a comparable position as I was. Is this proof of discrimination in employment? There were no discriminatory admission policies at my college—yet there were no black students in my class who had declared an accounting major. When I sat for the CPA exam, there were no policies that discriminated against minorities to explain why out of the thousands of people taking the exam, only a handful were minorities. The only prerequisite you had to meet to sit for the exam was that you had to have achieved a bachelor's degree in accounting. I took a pre-CPA exam study course I obtained through the mail. Anyone with a few bucks could buy those same books and tapes. When I sat in night school for four years while working long hours as a staff person in public accounting—there was no prohibition against minority students that kept the chair next to me occupied by another white person. I see the absence of blacks in the tax consulting/accounting profession more as an indicator that blacks don't want my job or a truly comparable job, rather than an indicator of repressive discrimination.

David, I don't see the ball and chain on your ankle that slowed you down. You got the education you wanted and needed to succeed in your profession. If you had chosen a different profession, I have no doubt that you would be successful in that too.

Have I had everything handed to me on a silver spoon because I am a white man? My ancestors were farmers who fled the Netherlands, West Prussia, and finally the Ukraine because of religious persecution. My grandparents provided for their family as best that they could. Sometimes the best included living in an abandoned railroad car and wearing clothes made out of old feed bags. My parents continued that tradition of sacrificing for the next generation and providing the best that they could. Our family was a two-income family before it became commonplace. It took the wages of both my father and mother to provide for our family of four, even though we lived rent free in a parsonage.

I'm not looking for pity or sympathy, just trying to answer the question: Do you and I have equality of opportunity in this country today? I propose that we do. Our equality is the opportunity for an education, an education that gives us the necessary knowledge to obtain a job, a job that cannot be denied to either of us because of our race or gender. We have the equality to obtain the opportunity. It is what we do with the opportunities that present themselves to us that determines whether we will be successful. Does everybody start at the same point in the race? No, but that's a fact of life. Reality is that you start where the cards have been dealt and you run the race from there as best you can. When I graduated from college, I had one job offer. It was for an accounting firm I had never heard of, but they gave me a chance.

I don't see the tangible or intangible ball and chain around the legs of African Americans that prevents you from successfully running the race of life. Let me rephrase—I don't see the ball and chain of racist rejection of opportunity. There may be other balls and chains, but those we all have to live with.

Have I been given my jobs and opportunities because I am a white man? I honestly believe that I have the job I have today because God has blessed me, because my parents and grandparents made sacrifices so that I could achieve more than they, and because I have counted the cost and paid the price to earn the opportunities that I have before me.

As far as the issue of justice: The intent of my letter, and this one too, is not to state "Because I experience pain, you should too." I don't wish pain on anyone, least of all myself. But to quote a line from one of my favorite movies, "Life is pain."

Yes, we as Christians are to behave justly, compassionately, and sensitively, for that is how God calls us to live. Correct me if I'm wrong, but nowhere in the Scriptures does God say that it is our right to receive justice, compassion, mercy, fairness, or equality.

America is the land of opportunity. A child born in the Kennedy family may have more opportunities than you or I, but we still have access to opportunity. Opportunities come from education.

BZ

Brent,

*I*n your last letter you stated: "Correct me if I'm wrong, but nowhere in the Scriptures does God say that it is our right to receive justice, compassion, mercy, fairness, or equality." Is it not true that God desires us to live in an environment where people receive justice, compassion, mercy, fairness, or equality? Or do we just think that God commanded us as Christians to live this way but not to really attain it? Is it His desire that I preach compassion in my church but tell my congregants not to expect to receive it? Should we tell our children that God is a God of justice but that we should not expect to receive justice? Of course you would agree that this is absurd. However, you or I don't claim these "rights." As Christians we claim our status as "slaves" to a heavenly master who commands us to live out the character qualities and attributes mentioned above.

Regarding your family struggle, I appreciate the pain and toil your family went through and I surely don't want to minimize your experience. In fact I admire it.

Obviously our professions determine our salary ranges. But I challenge you to compare your salary with the black man who is an accountant in your office and see what the variation is. That would be an interesting comparison to see if a black and white of similar position and training were earning comparable salaries. Is it really fair to say: "Black man or woman, just because your salaries are lower and the glass ceiling structures in corporate America are real, deal with it because we all struggle and life is pain"? I don't believe it is.

You see, Brent, it is easy for the advantaged to say to the disadvantaged, "Get with the program, suck it up, and be responsible." This is where sensitivity, compassion, and equality must come in. I agree that life may not have been served to you on a silver platter, but can you deny that there are advantages and preferential treatment for those who are white in this country?

Are we really equal? Read the following excerpt taken from Ray Hartman's writings in The Riverfront Times regarding preferential treatment and see another perspective:

Of the nation's airplane pilots, 98.3 percent are white.
Of the nation's geologists, 95.9 percent are white.
Of the nation's dentists, 95.6 percent are white.
Of the nation's authors, 93.9 percent are white.
Of the nation's lawyers, 93.8 percent are white.
Of the nation's aerospace engineers, 93.8 percent are white.
Of the nation's economists, 91.9 percent are white.
Of the nation's architects, 90.6 percent are white.
We live in a largely white country. The white majority enjoys a disproportionate share of its wealth and comfort and an even greater share of control over most of its institutions. But white power is so pervasive that it's never perceived, or even considered, white power. It's just the way things are. Racial percentages aren't tallied from the white side, only from the "minority" point of view. Thus, when 20 percent of public contracts on a building project are "set aside" for minority contractors, it is a "racial" or "gender-based" issue, but when 100 percent goes to firms owned by white males, it's just, well, reality. Even many sympathetic

to blacks and other people of color will find it quite reasonable that whites have 80-something or 90-something percent dominance of important institutions.

After all, the country is 80 percent white, so the statistics are always going to seem racially tilted toward Caucasians, right?

Well, not exactly. Only 37 percent of the nation's jail inmates were white in 1994 (as compared with 56 percent in 1978), and only 46 percent of the prisoners executed in the past six decades were white. In the same way that numbers can swing disproportionately white, so it is possible for whites to be under-represented statistically.

You see, Brent, I doubt if the issue of equality is as cut-and-dry as you may think. To tell a man to "pull himself up by his own bootstraps" when he doesn't have boots is not compassionate. To tell a man to "pull himself up by his own bootstraps" when one hand is tied behind his back is not equality.

Regarding you and me? Yes, you are correct, we do have equal opportunity in many areas. For that I am thankful. However, I believe the issue is deeper than just you and me. You and I are more alike than different. Both our dads were pastors. Both of us went to Christian colleges. However, had my college not been sensitive to increasing their black enrollment, I would not have made it in. I didn't have good academics to make it into college, but they admitted me and gave me an opportunity. They were sensitive to the imbalance of black students and had to intentionally make extra efforts to enroll blacks because they realized that without intentionality, inequality and/or imbalance would always exist.

I am thankful that my alma mater took a chance on me because the extra effort helped me and allowed me to prove myself. It was there that I became the first black president of the freshman class and then the first black president of the student body. A few years after graduating, I became the first black president of the board of directors for the Alumni Association. Now I am pastoring a young and thriving multicultural church that I founded.

I am not boasting; I am blessed! I'm blessed because a white institution gave me an opportunity because they realized that inequality and imbalance exist. I am forever grateful for my school's investment in me—a black man. Do not think for a minute, my brother, that their actions were unintentional. Neither will rectifying the playing field of inequality and imbalance be.

Brent, the reason why you don't see the invisible ball and chain on my ankle is because, by God's grace, it was cut off by this Christian college when they decided to give me a break. The reason why you do not see the glass ceiling in your corporation is because it doesn't exist for you. As a result, it is difficult for you to even comprehend why many more blacks do not move up corporate ladders as quickly and smoothly as you are able to. Therefore, you think that minorities must not be interested in your profession, your company, or your work ethic. Nothing could be further from the truth.

What is true, however, is that you have not had the "equal opportunity" I have had to be stopped by four different police officers in one day for driving through a nice suburban neighborhood to my new job. You don't have the "equal opportunity" of salespeople glaring at you in suspicion of you stealing something in grocery and clothing stores. You don't have the "equal opportunity" of men and women lunging for their car door locks when you near their vehicle, nor do you feel compelled to leave really big tips at restaurants to prove that you are not a "cheap" black person. You probably haven't experienced the opportunity of being passed up by cab drivers. The greatest of equal opportunity experiences that I have had most recently was when a white businessman gave me a free deal over the telephone because he mistakenly thought I was white like him. I refused to correct him as he continually disclosed his disdain for minorities in business who get free handouts, are irresponsible workers, and don't have business minds, as he put it.

My desire is that you, my brother, will never have such "equal opportunity!"

DA

David,

I am beginning to think we may be unable to reconcile our differences of opinion on this topic but I'm not ready to give up yet.

Please understand that I will continue to be offended by the assertion that just because I am white, I have been handed everything on a silver platter or even that I have been advantaged. Why does this offend me? Because it diminishes the efforts and sacrifices I have made to merely get myself into a position where "success" is a possibility for me. To say that I have been advantaged says it wasn't necessary for me to study hard in high school, college, or graduate school. It says that the 300 hours I studied for the CPA exam were unnecessary, that the 60–80-hour busy-season workweeks I put in during my six years in public accounting were unnecessary. And it says that my four years in night school to obtain my graduate degree were all a waste. Why were these efforts unnecessary and a waste? Because I am an "advantaged" white male and all white males are guaranteed to be successful and live life on easy street.

You say you don't believe that "life is pain." Maybe our difference here is semantics, but for me, it is the struggle and "the pain" that provide the satisfaction in achieving a goal. You say it is insensitive for me to tell blacks "get with the program, suck it up, and be responsible." Why shouldn't I tell that to others? At least once a week I tell myself some variation of those same words. Why do I do this? Because I strive to discipline myself, push myself, and challenge myself so that I may be a good tax accountant, a valued employee, a promise keeper of a husband, and a good neighbor. It's not always easy, it's not always fun—but I keep focused on my goals and accept the struggle and "pain."

Why do whites dislike affirmative action? Why do I dislike affirmative action? I dislike any "program" that rewards people for underachievement. I especially dislike the attitude of "I personally am entitled to be exempted from the standards applicable to others because my parents and ancestors were discriminated against." Does there need to be a greater representation of minorities in "white-collar" professions? Sure, and I am willing to support such a goal— if the increased minority representation is comprised of fully qualified persons. You want the position, then you get the necessary knowledge, skills, and qualifications—no exceptions.

You stated that you didn't have sufficient academics to get into your college but that they admitted you anyway. I am assuming that you mean you didn't have good enough grades. If this is true, then you got lucky. You had the opportunity during grade school and high school to be a good student and get good grades and obtain entry into a college solely on your own academic merits. You almost blew it, but your college gave you a second chance and you demonstrated that you were worthy of that chance.

You were given an opportunity you didn't personally deserve (you didn't have the grades) and instead of claiming that opportunity as your right because your ancestors were enslaved, you seized the opportunity to prove yourself worthy and qualified, and you graduated feeling blessed and grateful. Thank you for your attitude of gratitude.

You say it is not compassionate of me to say to blacks, "Pull yourself up by your own bootstraps." Did you have one hand tied behind your back when you pulled yourself up by your own bootstraps and seized upon your second chance at college? What are "the boots" and the "bootstraps"?—the drive and will to struggle and prove yourself worthy of other opportunities.

You propose that I am blind to a glass ceiling simply because I am a white male. You state that "nothing could be further from the truth" as to my statement that blacks do not appear to desire a tax accounting career. Then help me comprehend why blacks are not flooding into the colleges and public accounting firms to obtain the specific education and training needed for a comparable career.

In spite of what you think—I am not advocating or justifying a race-based or gender-based inequality. And although the point is not worthy of further argument—when we get to heaven let's ask the first-century Christians, the seventeenth-century Anabaptists, and the twentieth-century believers behind the old Iron Curtain if they received justice, compassion, mercy, fairness, or equality. David, human rights (which I believe in and am all for) are a privilege and are not guaranteed even by God. As Christians we are to practice justice, compassion, mercy, fairness, and equality in our daily lives—even if all we receive in return is persecution, slavery, or death.

I don't know if I have turned up the heat or toned down the discussion by this letter. I guess you'll let me know. So do we have an impasse of opinion on equality and equal opportunity?

BZ

Brent,

You asked, "So do we have an impasse of opinion on equality and equal opportunity?" Probably. We may have to agree to disagree. It is difficult for me to believe, though, that you cannot understand and admit that whites have an unfair advantage in this country where whites hold the power and the purse strings. I can see that it is hard for you to separate being "advantaged" from the fact that you have had to struggle and work hard in life. These two ideas are not diametrically opposed. Just because someone has an advantage doesn't mean that everything is handed to them on a silver platter and that they haven't worked hard. I admire your hard work and the work of your family.

I will agree with you that "life is pain" at times but I don't believe that it is fair to say to blacks "because life is pain, deal with inequality." God calls you and me to help others who are downtrodden, disadvantaged, and who need a "hand up" not just a handout. I will continue to preach the message of compassion because this is what God has called us to. I'm sure if I were to ask the Christians persecuted over the centuries if life was fair, compassionate, and equal in their times that they would surely say "no." But was their persecution at the hands of other Christ-followers or at the hands of evil, racist, and bigoted men?

Life isn't easy all the time for anyone, but this should not justify inequality or a lack of fairness. Christ calls us to help those who are the last, the least, the lost, and the left out. I challenge you to think about these issues of compassion.

I do not have a problem separating the issues of advantage and hard work. Nor do I have a problem separating the issues of affirmative action and helping "qualified minorities." Do not assume the only reason blacks have not risen up the employment ranks to be because they are unqualified. Nor should we assume that those who have risen in such fields have done so solely because of an "affirmative action placement" of an unqualified person.

Although I believe that affirmative action needs an overhaul, please know that there is great merit for those who can say, "Because we were a part of the problem for many, many years, now we will be part of the solution for years to come." Anything less is a refusal to take responsibility.

When I hurt my knee in football as a teenager, I realized how difficult life can be for disabled people. Even to this day my knee pops out every now and then causing me to use crutches and reminding me how difficult it can be for the disabled. When I have had to crutch my way up steps because there was no elevator in the building, I have been reminded of the difficulty of being disabled. As a fully functioning, athletic, and mobile male, my sensitivity is almost nonexistent to the world of the handicapped. Whenever I reinjure my knee, it is then that I remember why there are handicapped parking spaces and the like. Here's my point: As Christians we should be sensitive to help those who are in need. Although disabled people should not whine or have a chip on their shoulder (and I don't know of any who do), they should expect kindness to prevail in others when help is needed. It is not their right, it is just a hope that human kindness exists in some measure. This is why we give them first choice at parking spaces. This is why we install special stalls in bathrooms. Unfortunately human kindness doesn't exist in great measure; therefore laws must be established to help the callous of heart comply. As the disabled have a physical inequality that we would all agree needs to be equalized by the law, affirmative action has served as a legal equalizer for blacks in the workplace.

It is very difficult for the advantaged to see the advantages they receive. As a white male, you are privileged whether you know it or not. This doesn't discount your hard work, but one day I hope you will recognize that you have the "home court" advantage. Oh, if you could only walk in my shoes for a while, my brother. If you could come play life on my court. Not because I'm boohooing and desiring sympathy for I have been truly blessed. But for your sake, so that you can see what life is like when a black man, who works as hard as you have to get where you are, is rejected because of the color of his skin, and not the content of his character or the qualifications of his work.

If you are right, that no racial advantage or racial inequality exist, then the implication is that blacks are lazy, shiftless, irresponsible whiners who do not have the mental or intellectual ability to ascend to professional or white-collar professions. Just as you are offended by the implication that your hard work was unnecessary for you as a white man to be successful, blacks are offended by the implication I just mentioned. Let me reiterate a statement I made earlier. Blacks are not looking for simple equality per se. Blacks are looking for justice, fairness, and the same equal access as whites. Blacks are looking for a level playing field.

DA

Why do I have to call you "African American"?

This question and the following question deal with racial identity and culture. If you are a nonblack reader, these next two groupings of letters will take you into an arena you may never get to enter in person, for the African American culture in this country is a cherished and protected component of identity. The important thing for nonblack readers here is not to agree or disagree, like or dislike the culture or labels blacks have created for themselves. The important thing is for whites and others to better understand the cultural identity of the black individual they think they know and understand.

David,

*T*here is a lot of talk these days about black identity and culture, how important your own race's identity and culture are, and how offensive and insensitive whites are to this identity and culture. To be honest, I have absolutely no idea what black identity and black culture are. In fact I would be surprised if more than a handful of whites across the country have a handle on it either.

Since there is so much importance placed on these concerns, please help me understand what this identity and culture are. Unless you tell me, I have no recourse but to find my definitions from the media and I doubt that is the place you would like me to find answers.

I want to share with you one example of whites' frustrations in attempting to understand black identity. You probably have noticed in our letters so far that I have consistently described your race as "black" and not as "African American." This has been intentional.

The label "African American" appears to be the latest in a string of politically correct labels for a race of people who apparently have an identity crisis and are unable to define who they are. "Negro," "colored," "black," "Afro-American," "African American"—what's next? I have no idea where the label "Negro" came from. "Colored" and "black" are more obvious, even though "colored" couldn't be used today because it no longer implies black, there are many people of a variety of skin tones in this country today. However, I have a problem with "African American" and any national combination hyphenated with "American."

If the person being described is a "dual citizen" of another country and the United States or the person himself immigrated to the United States, then it seems logical to identify the person as Korean-American, African-American, Swedish-American, etc. The logic comes from that person himself having cultural and physical ties to both places due to having lived in both countries for an extended time. For example, it makes sense to identify a woman as a Korean-American if she was born in Korea, lived in Korea as a child, and speaks Korean. On the other hand it doesn't make any sense to refer to my father as a Swiss-American because he was born and raised in this country, speaks only English, and it was his grandfather who emigrated from Switzerland.

Let's be honest here—my only ties to Switzerland are that it is the homeland of my ancestors. Yes, I would like to go visit there, and yes, I feel a special affection for the country because my roots are traceable there. But the United

States of America is my homeland and my country and this is where I choose to live.

Your only ties to Africa are that it is the homeland of your ancestors. Yes, I would expect that you would like to visit there, and yes, I would expect that you would have a special affection for that land because your roots are traceable there. But the United States of America is your homeland, your country, and this is where you personally have chosen to live.

My passport like your passport identifies us both as Americans. The melting pot has been discarded and our country has splintered into little or large ethnic groups who want to live in America but not adopt or help mold American culture. Whether people like you or don't like you because of your race, you are still an American and your culture is American. Assume there was no pigmentation to your skin or my skin or anyone's skin, I would expect an independent observer to say, "DA, Brent, you both act American, enjoy things that Americans typically enjoy, you dress in typically American clothing, you appreciate fine arts that Americans typically enjoy, you celebrate the 4th of July, you like baseball, basketball, football, and apple pie, you identify the President of the United States as your national leader—you are both American."

Yet blacks that were born and raised only in America want to identify themselves as not just Americans but also Africans. I do not understand. I'm not trying to be offensive or insensitive. I just do not understand how whites are supposed to be able to understand and recognize the culture and identity of blacks living in America if the very self-identifying label of this group of people changes every generation. Blacks desire equality and acceptance, but yet insist on identifying themselves with a label (African American) that is somewhat divisive and not unifying between races.

One last note about my discussion on "African American." I was sitting in the chair of the woman who cuts my hair every month. I do not know how she got on the topic. I said nothing to initiate it nor did I comment on what she said.

Some of my comments in the above paragraphs were directly out of her mouth, particularly the passport comment. The woman is from Jamaica and yes she is black. She refuses to let her friends force her to use the "African American" label. She was adamant in stating that she is an American of Jamaican descent. She didn't call herself Jamaican-American, though I think she would have the right to do so having lived in both countries. She calls herself an American; she just happens to have skin pigmentation that is black.

Once again, the issue of this letter is not which label is used to identify your race, but rather what is the identity and culture of the African American race?

BZ

Brent,

*A*llow me to summarize what I perceive your letter to be asking: What is black identity and culture and why use the term African American to distinguish yourselves?

The melting pot of the United States doesn't simply mean to blend into the same pot bringing together only color differences. The melting pot means the bringing together of color and culture, whether by intent or default.

To ask those from China, Japan, Africa, Spain, India, etc. to come to America, check their heritage and culture at the customs counter, and then move on into American life is unrealistic.

No matter how many generations pass, heritage will always affect those who are connected with their backgrounds, especially if they are brought up having their heritage emphasized in the home. (Allow me to interject that it is unacceptable for culture to be used as an excuse not to learn English or not to submit one's allegiance to America.)

Much heritage and culture in America is taught and retained through family and oral tradition. However, the further one's generation is removed from their genesis in this country, the more watered-down their culture becomes. It is at this point that many second- and third-generation citizens of America struggle internally regarding their identity. Many lose or let go of their culture, while others hang onto their cultural heritage with every fiber in their body. Then there are several in between who have learned to balance their cultural identity well.

As a result of such cultural integration, you have ethnic towns, restaurants, churches, music, accents, and languages. The home you grow up in will either accentuate or dilute such distinctions. Black Americans of African descent are no different. Culturally we have our distinct clothing, hairstyles, food, music, churches, and "lingo."

Notice I said "black Americans of African descent." To identify this group as "black" wouldn't suffice because it would not include your Jamaican friend mentioned in your letter, nor would it include any other group with black skin who would not fit into the above name. I could have said "Americans," but that doesn't help anyone when we are trying to identify different kinds of Americans. I could have said "Africans," but that isn't true because black Americans are not African citizens. They are American citizens of African descent. Perhaps a better way of identifying this group is African American.

Let me be the first to say that whether someone is Swiss American or African American doesn't change the fact that we are all American! This is where we'd agree. However, I think that we also agree that there is a need to distinguish different American groups. In fact, if this need were not the case, there would not even be a distinction between "white" and "black" Americans now.

So I think that terms must be used to help us distinguish one another. Then we must ask the question, "What shall the terms be and who shall designate them?"

This is where I think the term "African American" came from. For the first time black Americans of African descent had the opportunity to name themselves. For the first time in our history it wasn't the slave master who named us, but we were naming ourselves. Names like "nigger, spook, colored, black" were all imposed upon us. With new freedom came the opportunity for newness across the board. As black Americans of African descent (it's easier to say African Americans or blacks, so from this point on, I will) continue to learn who they are, where they came from, and what their cultural heritage is, they will continue to grow into an identity; the very thing that was lost in slavery.

After preaching in the Bahamas this past weekend, I can totally see how different the blacks are over there compared to blacks here. I can finally understand Michelle Gardner, a Bahamian who is in our church. Blacks over there are in power. Blacks over there make up the vast majority of the country. Blacks over there are totally separated from the whites who have money.

Michelle Gardner is racially black but culturally Bahamian. And there is a huge difference. Their history is totally different. The way they see themselves is different. They have an identity. They know who they are. They are not "striving," "struggling," or trying to gain equality. They aren't born disadvantaged or thought ill of because of their color. The greatest advantage/disadvantage there is being born in a family that is rich or poor.

On the other hand, some in the Bahamas look down on the Haitians believing that they are only good for one thing: gardening. Black Bahamians, Americans, and Haitians may all look alike, but culturally, they are all as different as their countries.

My point is this: Identity goes further than names, color, or titles of citizenship. To be American is much more than apple pie and baseball. Being American is bringing your cultural heritage (be it European, German, Jewish, or Swiss) into a melting pot. This is better labeled a "mixed bag!"—which can be defined as a bunch of foreigners, immigrants, and natives who want to live in freedom under a common constitution and government.

This "mixed bag" needs governing and leadership in order for such an experiment to work. Civil wars will be inevitable if leadership doesn't arise to bring unity from all factions. Be it whites in the Midwest or blacks in L.A. or Hispanics in Miami.

I must add that leadership has arisen in Christendom. His name is Jesus Christ and He unifies us. Thus within the church, we must follow His leadership! We must settle for nothing less than complete unity (John 17:23)!

Unfortunately I do not believe that there is much hope for those outside of the church beyond keeping the lid on angry and volcanic expressions, such as through sensitivity training and moral appeals. There will always be Bosnias, Rwandas, Iraqs, and Americas. Christianity is the purest of melting pots!

I personally do not care whether someone calls me black or African American because I use them synonymously. It is like David or DA. One name may be more appropriate given the audience or company I'm in, but it really doesn't matter beyond that.

You will always have extremists who will make an issue with one side of the coin or the other. I think sensitivity and appropriateness are key. It is unfortunate that political correctness has extended itself beyond reason. It is equally unfortunate, however, that the rebellion against political correctness has extended itself beyond sensitivity.

In conclusion, let me write a separate document on black culture if this writing doesn't suffice. I listed the general areas of culture where people differ. If you would like me to specify those differences, I will await some specific question according to those ideas.

I hope this was helpful, brother!

DA

What is African American culture?

David,

*W*ell stated, my friend. I expect you'll be seeing me use the term "African American" more often now in our writings.

In my letter I asked you to define the culture of African Americans. You very deftly mentioned some of the components of culture and then totally stayed away from the topic. I don't blame you at all; it was probably an unfair question because neither one of us is a sociologist. However, if I can force the issue, I would appreciate your insight on African American culture.

BZ

Brent,

*A*llow me to explain culture this way: Culture is a contextual influence and environment that shapes and molds one's thinking and livelihood based on one's family heritage, racial history, upbringing, language, expressions, looks, and needs.

When a child is born into a family context, his values, language, family heritage, and memories are all shaped very early on. As the child grows up, he is shaped by the broader context of his environment (i.e., school, TV, relatives,

81

friends, music, etc.). As a child absorbs all of these influences into his mind, his way of thinking and relating is directly connected to what he has learned and experienced within and outside of the home. (Comment: this is why it is so important for Christians to "renew their minds" and learn how to think biblically, as we are "born again" into a new family culture called "the church.")

Blacks, Hispanics, whites, Asians, Jews, Native Americans, etc. all bring different aspects of their culture to the melting pot of America.

Remember, you are not born with a trait called "culture." You are brought up within the context of a culture, which includes heritage, history, upbringing, language, expression, looks, and needs. For example:

HERITAGE—Blacks have a family heritage that is ethnocentric. There is great pride in the struggle from which our existence in America has been born. Often there are many extended family members, but little financial interdependence. The spiritual and social tradition of the black church has been the hub and soul of our community.

HISTORY—Blacks have a history that is rooted in oppression producing much anguish, grief, and distrust. Music is a strong anchor in the history of blacks. Strong women have often been the backbone and at the forefront of black leadership. The black man is still confused about his identity and often struggles with his self-concept.

UPBRINGING—Just as many Jewish people are brought up learning to eat kosher foods, many blacks are brought up, generally speaking, with certain foods cooked in a certain way. Some have called it soul food. Blacks tend to grow up with a religious connection to the church, which emphasizes some black heroes and holidays.

LANGUAGE—American whites usually only have American English as a language, while other nationalities and races around the world typically are fluent in multiple languages. As the American youth culture uses a slightly different vocabulary when communicating with one another, so do many blacks. Blacks have slang or an American English dialect that is used throughout different pockets of the black community. However, the primary language and primary emphasis in this country is American English.

EXPRESSION—People from different cultural backgrounds express themselves differently. Not only in the ways they communicate, but in the style of clothes, hair, music, and other preferences. We cannot box every individual into a group and say that they must all like a particular style of clothing, hair, or music. But we can notice general patterns of styling preferences among Hispanics, Asians, Native Americans, African Americans, and whites, regarding some of these areas. We must be warned again never to place anyone in a box because we are all different as individuals and we live in the great American "melting pot," which allows us to mix and match all of our different experiences and styles. This is what makes multiculturalism so beautiful.

LOOKS—We all look different. Each ethnic group has similar features, which allow them to identify with each other as well as identify those who are different than themselves. The differing features include skin color, nose shape, eye shape, body build, hair texture, etc. This can be a very positive thing, especially in the body of Christ where we celebrate and embrace our uniqueness, designed by the fingers of our Creator. Unfortunately these features have been used for divisiveness in our world and are often at the front line and forefront of discrimination. As Christians, we must deny such prejudice on every hand. Instead, we must celebrate and encourage unity by proactively and intentionally assuring that we are not excluding but including those who represent our church body. If these distinctions weren't connected to culture (which they often are but not always), and if these distinctions weren't so pronounced visibly (which is a part of God's great design), then we wouldn't have to think about balancing our government, corporations, or management teams. But we do! Why? Because diversity is seen first, then experienced.

Unfortunately people are still judged negatively by the color of their skin instead of the content of their character. Therefore we must assure that everyone has the equal opportunities that the majority race has.

Racial reconciliation is so important within the church of Jesus Christ because it takes these visual distinctions that have separated many in this culture for centuries and fuels the worship of a creative Deity. When we as Christians make an intentional effort to demonstrate to the world that blacks and whites can serve "side by side" and "heart-to-heart" together for Christ, it becomes a powerful witness to an onlooking and divided world. The greatest division in American culture is between black and white because of this country's history. Therefore, as racial reconciliation is realized between these extremes in America (black and white), it will be a visible witness to our community and will draw in other minority cultures as well.

NEEDS—I am reminded of the fact that my needs as a black man are different than those of my white friends. Albeit our basic needs are the same, specifically, the process of meeting those needs is different. For example, whites and blacks have a need to care for their hair, but the way they care for their hair is different. I went to six different well-known mainline stores in the Columbia, Maryland, area and I could not find a brush for my "black" hair. This is one of the most integrated communities in the country. I was outraged. I could not believe that these stores had nothing for my needs as a black man. Thus there becomes a need for a specialized store for black beauty products. That is where I ended up.

In the same vein, when it comes to news and information that affect black people, I will not find it in the mainstream media. Thus there becomes a need for specialized magazines, news material, businesses, etc. Sometimes whites have questioned me about such specialized organizations, business groups, and periodicals. I remind them that such organizations are born out of America's lack of proactivity and intentionality to fairly assimilate black Americans into the mainstream of American life. Thus specialized organizations are born. Remember, I can't even get a common hair product in one of the most integrated communities in the country.

Every culture has its own set of needs that must be met.

Conclusion: Brent, you and I have many of the same needs as Americans and as men. We have the same needs as human beings. But because of background and culture there are some differences. That is not bad; it is good. We should grow to know and love each other for who we are and celebrate whatever differences we have. Our diversity is a tribute to the Creator.

But remember, with regard to culture, blacks know a whole lot more about whites than vice versa. We as blacks have to know how to live among white America in order to make it in this world. But what about you? Have you stepped out to learn about my culture? In all honesty, most whites have not. They really don't care. As long as I assimilate into the white American culture, I can succeed and be accepted.

Is it right to ask a black man to put away his music, clothing, food, special needs, and culture to assimilate? Can whites and blacks be on the road to reconciliation if one group says, "I'll reconcile and accept you as long as you don't bring your culture, names, leaders, music, or ethnicity with you?" Is that racial reconciliation or a sophisticated way of repeating the heinous history of this country?

When it comes to racial reconciliation, white people must decide to move toward blacks and their culture to show an interest and a desire to learn.* Most blacks will respond well to this and unbelievable bridges can be built as a result.

DA

*One of the best ways to build bridges is to demonstrate the attitude of a learner. When developing a relationship with a person from a different background, just ask questions. Ask about their culture, upbringing, beliefs, and struggles. This attitude of learning will begin to lead you down the road of reconciliation.

Is Black English okay?

Language is an integral component of culture, whether it is American culture or African American culture. For minority groups in this country, language is one of the most cherished components of their culture. For whites, the failure of minorities to embrace, adopt, and master the Standard English language—all the while claiming to be victims of inequality—is beyond comprehension and becomes a line in the sand dividing our races at an impasse. The following discussion does not address the appropriateness of either dialect of English but rather the consequences to the minority of not mastering Standard English. Then we ask, Who bears the responsibility for these consequences?

———

David,

*B*efore we leave the topic of culture I would like to spend some time talking about the language component. I have attached two articles from the Chicago Tribune that were printed on consecutive days last December. The articles were part of a series following the everyday life of a single, African American mother of three living in the Chicago housing projects. At the end of this paragraph, before you continue reading this letter, I ask that you read both articles. The first is titled "Earning Another Chance" and the second is "Hopes on Hold."* There are many possible discussions we could have about Andrea Wellington's life and her experiences, just from what we read in these articles. I want to focus, though, on the side effects the language of her culture had on her ability to change her economic situation for herself and her children. First, read the articles; then we'll continue.

In your letter, one of the components of culture you mentioned was "lingo." I assume you would define lingo as being terms, phrases, statements, references, and words that are common to a particular group of people. Surfers have lingo; deadheads have lingo; hackers have lingo; athletes have lingo; even Christians have a lingo. I think I had always known there was a lingo of the street and even an African American lingo but I hadn't really thought that either of these were pervasive enough to warrant a classification of "Black American English" (as presented in the article), a separate dialect, originating from "Standard English," still similar, yet significantly different.

After reading the articles and thinking about their implications, I began to look at what appeared to me to be side effects of our two groups speaking different dialects of English.

Language is a learned ability. Children learn to speak the language of their parents and their community. Two babies born on the same day in different countries will speak different languages. It has nothing to do with racial genetics but everything to do with environment. As children, we learn to speak our language long before we are able to write it and we are able to write words long before we are able

*See articles in the 29 December 1994 and 30 December 1994 issues of the *Chicago Tribune*.

to assemble those words into sentences and paragraphs that generally follow the "rules" of the language.

To an extent, a person's mastery of the "rules" of the standard language of their country is dependent upon the person's education. However, education isn't the exclusive answer. Andrea Wellington not only had a high school education, she had a college education too. Yet she had significant problems writing in Standard English. Why did she have these problems? The answer seems to me that Standard English was never made a priority in the environment she grew up in as a child, nor in the neighborhood she resided in as an adult. What language was given priority? Apparently Black American English.

What was the genesis of Black American English and why has it been perpetuated to the extent that it has when those who embrace it appear to be limiting their economic advancement?

People advance themselves economically generally because of or through employment. The official language of international businesses is English, Standard English. A person, or group of people, have the choice to speak any language or variation of a language they choose. However, such a person, of any race, has to realize that if they choose not to develop basic skills and abilities in the standard language of the country they live in, that if they for any reason choose a different language or a dialect of the standard, that many of their options and opportunities to succeed will have been limited by their own choices.

Not all African Americans struggle with writing or speaking Standard English. From what I've been able to observe, inner-city blacks appear to struggle more than others do. Why? Perhaps education, but I think it is the community and the choices the community makes as to whether it will speak the dialect or the standard.

BZ

Brent,

You inquired as to the "genesis" of "Black American English." The roots go back to slavery. The African slaves were taught the minimum amount of English they would need to communicate with and understand the commands of their masters. As the second and third generation of slaves and children of former slaves were born, the native language of their ancestors was forgotten. Yet the education of "Negroes" and "colored" people never became a priority until post–Civil War. It is conventional wisdom that a student is unable to progress beyond the knowledge or abilities of their teacher. It is no surprise then that absent deliberate education, the generations following slavery would only learn the limited, broken English of their parents and grandparents.

Sometime after the civil rights movement two things changed. Basic education from kindergarten through high school became available to all persons regardless of race. Blacks could no longer be denied an education merely because they were black. Secondly, a distinct identity and culture became a priority to blacks as their passion to gain freedoms, equality, and civil rights grew. Blacks wanted to be different from whites, to have their own identity, and to have their own culture that honored their African ancestors and heritage. As African Americans developed this identity and culture, the broken English and street lingo unofficially evolved into the standard language of the culture and became the dialect called Black American English.

In my opinion, this dialect has continued because of poor schooling and lowered expectation. There is nothing wrong with having a cultural dialect as long as the standard language is also mastered so these kids can succeed when they get older. I agree with you, Brent, that black children (all children) ought to be taught proper English and it should be a priority. But let's remember where the federal and state dollars go. When it comes to paying teachers, dispersing money to certain schools in certain counties, what schools do you think get cheated? What school systems do you think get the best teachers? Oftentimes the poor city schools have crummy facilities and equipment, while in the suburban schools, the facilities are nicer, and the latest in equipment and computers is readily available.

My point is this: If we are going to take the challenge of educating our children seriously, then we need to put our money where our mouth is and invest it in the poorer school systems so the children who are not fortunate enough to be in the nicer schools can have the same opportunity to learn and grow.

Of course the parents must be involved also if children are going to succeed in school. You and I both know that the breakdown of the family unit among black America is epidemic. The black home is another subject all together, but it affects education. Personally, I think the black home should be the number one concern and area of concentration of our black organizations.

So then I end with a quote from your last letter followed by a rhetorical, and hopefully, thought-provoking question: "However, such a person, of any race, has to realize that if they choose not to develop basic skills and abilities in the standard language of the country they live in, that if they for any reason choose a different language or a dialect of the standard, that many of their options and opportunities to succeed will have been limited by their own choices."

Can we truly say that it is solely the responsibility of these black children to educate themselves to speak Standard English?

DA

David,

Here are my thoughts on your thought-provoking rhetorical question.

The responsibility can lie only in the teachers or the students or the community in which both live.

The teachers, the home, and the community all have to work together to educate our children. But who has the ultimate responsibility to learn? The student. The old saying applies: "You can lead a horse to water but you can't make him drink." We could build the most glorious structures, filled with the latest in technology, staffed by the brightest minds in the world—but if the student does not take the personal responsibility to learn the subject matter being taught, then all the investment in buildings and computers and teachers will have been wasted money.

Is it the responsibility of black students to learn to speak and write Standard English? If they have the opportunity to learn the skill—then yes it is their responsibility.

You don't need a computer or a beautiful school building to learn to speak and read and write. I propose that a qualified teacher equipped only with chalk and a chalkboard and textbooks, pencils, and paper for the students could teach a willing student to speak, read, and write Standard English.

I agree with you, we should allocate more resources to poorer school districts. We should help our children to learn and become skilled in any way we can. But the disparity in basic education wasn't created by money or the lack thereof, nor will it be solved by throwing money in the general direction of the problem. The theory that's out there is that students in poorer school districts perform worse than those in wealthier districts because of the disparity in spending by those districts. But how much money does it take to learn the grammar and structure of Standard English? I propose that it costs simply the price of a textbook and a teacher who insists that students learn the subject matter.

I agree that the education of our children, no matter where they reside, should be a priority for all of us. I would also agree that we should more deliberately allocate educational dollars to maximize the learning of all American children and not just the children in our own county or school district. However, I would disagree that a mere allocation of funds or purchasing of computers will equalize the disparities that exist on the standardized achievement tests between the districts.

What is the critical knowledge that must be obtained from kindergarten through high school? The three Rs: reading, writing, and arithmetic. The rest is nice, the rest is helpful, but the rest is not critical. What is the critical skill that must be obtained from kindergarten through high school? The ability to learn about a subject matter you previously did not know about, and the ability to apply that knowledge to life. Computer skills are nice for kids to have, and without those skills they are handicapped when competing in the marketplace. But you don't need a computer or any other type of electronic device to obtain the basics: the critical knowledge and skills that must be obtained by the time a person graduates from high school. If a person has computer skills but does not know or cannot use the grammatical basics, they will fail. If a person knows the basics, then even if they graduate high school without computer skills, they have the tools to succeed in life.

BZ

Brent,

*O*ne of the things I have learned from personal experience and from my classes on education is the importance environment has on the learning process. Yes, the student has his responsibility, but there are other factors involved in learning. Have you ever heard the old saying, "The teacher hasn't taught unless the student has learned"? You see, every student learns differently and teachers need to tune into how to motivate students to learn. But there are other variables that fit into this equation besides the teacher, learner, and environment. That is curriculum. Now this is a subject that many educators battle over and I don't feel the need to go down this road at this time. But please know that the curriculum and content along with the environment, teacher, and learner are crucial.

I have discussed such matters as these with teachers who have taught in various environments, and they have said that a child's parents are a critical part of the education process. A child who has involved parents will naturally do better in school. Many inner-city children don't have involved parents and many of them have to deal with many other life issues besides education. Therein lies the dilemma. The problems are there before the children get to the classroom, while they are in the classroom, and after they leave the classroom. All of this affects learning.

When you have dilapidated classrooms with no air conditioning or little heat in the winter, believe it or not, learning is affected. Can poor children make it against such odds? Sure, and many have, but isn't that just a little too much to ask from a kid? I think so. Is it fair and does it benefit society to have this "survival of the fittest" mentality with our children? This attitude is especially ironic when the people who are arguing the "survival of the fittest" position are the PhDs and politicians who have had the best learning, social, economic, and educational environments.

My point is simply this, Standard English should be taught, learned, and expected. However, it behooves us to rethink how we educate our children who are coming into our schools with broken lives, unsafe environments, and inadequate facilities.

DA

How do you react to public incidents of racism?

There continue to be racially motivated incidents in America that drive us back to our own perspectives regarding matters of race. In these letters we communicate about a couple of specific incidents that underscore the gulf between our perspectives. Whites and blacks often see through different lenses; these letters are prime examples of that. We both learned something about ourselves in this exchange.

David,

You've sent me two sets of newspaper articles recently. I have a request: no more articles without also sending your comments or perspective on what is being written. In the spirit of this request I am returning the article out of Jet magazine about the five racist high schoolers and I ask that you return it to me with your comments about what your reaction, as a black man, was when you read about these teens.*

To be fair, I'll give you my thoughts. I was initially saddened, probably mostly because I would like to believe that the white youth of today are not racist, that the bulk of white

*See article in the 2 June 1995 issue of *Jet* magazine.

racists are either the old guard who grew up in the days of "niggers" and "colored people" or the beer-guzzling good old boys who drape themselves in the American flag and defame any racial group but their own. I want to believe that suburbanites like myself and my family are not the perpetrators of racist ideology. It's articles like this that open my eyes to the truth, that it's not necessarily the "old guard" or "good old boys" that perpetrate racism among the generations—it's people who look a lot like me, maybe who even live in my same neighborhood.

Jail time for these high schoolers may seem harsh under the "no blood, no foul"* mentality, but I found myself agreeing that these boys need to be punished whether it be criminally or in the civil courts. Racist ideology needs to be confronted aggressively regardless of the perpetrator's race. An interesting "punishment," though, might be extended amounts of community service in an African American community.

Aside from my being saddened, the article didn't pull any emotional strings for me. It didn't anger me or even disgust me, and I think it should have. This lack of anger and disgust could probably be interpreted as condoning apathy, but I'm not convinced that is what I'm guilty of. Rather, I think the impetus is that the story doesn't affect me directly and unless I force the matter, the indirect effect would be almost imperceptible on my daily life. Secondly, the story simply didn't shock me enough to pull those emotional strings.

Lastly, I am left with a nagging question about this article. Did the publication of this news article in Jet magazine help promote racial reconciliation or did it foster divisiveness, bitterness, and hatred? Was the article edifying and necessary to be printed? In the right medium, I would say yes. I think Jet magazine, however, was the wrong medium

*This is a phrase used in pick-up games between athletes who know the rules of the game but don't want to slow down play unless an infraction is severe; thus, "no blood, no foul."

if the goal is to help increase awareness of racism and to help eliminate it. I am probably one of the few whites who will have read this article; the target market should have been whites not blacks. I would expect a black reader to have felt that this incident is just another brick in the wall between themselves and a hopelessly racist white America. White people need to read this article, not blacks. It should have been published in a periodical with a greater readership in the white community. Instead it was published where only those who are already convinced that racism exists will see it. This article could have been a tool to tear down racist ideology; instead I fear it was a tool to build up divisiveness, bitterness, and hatred.

BZ

Brent,

kay, you win, bro! No more articles without responses. I sent them with the hopes that they would provoke your thoughts and emotions untainted by my comments. However, I can see why you would like my response with the article.

About your response to the Jet article regarding the five high school seniors. I was somewhat shocked by it—your response that is. In my opinion, your response fell into the typical "white" reaction that blacks would expect, one that sadly admits that the incident is real yet fails to comprehend the overwhelming regularity and commonality of racism on every front. When you naively think that the "bulk of white racists are either the old guard who grew up in the days of niggers and colored people or the beer-guzzling good old boys who drape themselves in the American flag and defame any racial group but their own," you fall into the trap that many whites fall into. The trap of disbelief and pity.

Blacks have been saying for years that neighborhoods, the media, corporations, the criminal justice system, the police departments, the FBI, and the educational systems are racist by design or default. Usually these claims are met with a mixture of disbelief and pity. The angry white person shoots back with calling blacks hypersensitive and abusers of the "race card." Yes, there is a percentage of hypersensitive blacks and those who use the issue for personal gain, but this percentage of abusers should not discount the reality of racism in this country.

These five boys were not brought up in the South in the 1940s. These boys are teenagers and young adults who had to learn this sick form of hidden and covert racism. These boys represent a large percentage of their high school and community. They are simply the ones who had the "guts" to take the dare. These are the same boys who will go to Ivy League schools and matriculate into our legal system and corporations.

Regarding Jet magazine: I am thankful for such publications that inform me of that which the mainstream media doesn't cover unless the story is so big that it would make them look biased if they didn't.

Does this article feed anger in blacks? Of course! Should it not anger all of us? In fact there would be no need for the "special interest" magazines like Ebony, Jet, Black Enterprise, Essence, etc. if black interests were considered in America's mainstream media. Brent, when you open Time, Newsweek, People, Life, etc. tell me how many people of color you see. Tell me how many advertisements for my hair, my skin, my clothing, my art, my books, or my music you find. I am not talking about Michael Jackson, Jordan, Jesse, Colin Powell, or O. J. The media must cover these guys; they wouldn't be competitive if they didn't. They are forced to cover them. The times when blacks do get coverage is when—you guessed it—they commit crime.

Brent, I may sound angry, but passionate may be a more accurate representation. However, I cannot deny that there is some anger! Not at you, but at this system. You see, I firmly believe that the white community is an hour late and a dollar short on these issues. It's only after a long federal

97

investigation that "racist" issues surface to national attention (i.e., Denny's restaurants, Good ol' boys round up, etc.). Please know, my brother, that blacks don't respond to national reports on racism like this: "Gee, I'm saddened. I can't believe things are this way. I suppose it's an isolated incident. Oh well, let me go back to work." Blacks respond like this: "What's new!" And it's then that they respond angrily to their white neighbors who still don't get it. This anger turns into rage and then violence at times.

About the "no blood, no foul" rule. Blacks have been crying foul for a long time, with bandages all over their bodies, soaked in blood. And then the white referees come along in the fourth quarter, blow the whistle, and say, "I think I see a little blood—foul!" In the meantime, we've been suffering from external and internal bleeding for a long time!

When whites finally begin to see "blood" and begin to acknowledge racism, they may think that this comforts the black person and makes him happy—but it doesn't. It is only when the white person admits sorrowfully his or her embarrassingly elongated ignorance of the matter that the black begins to soften. When a referee says, "Oh gee . . . foul" in the fourth quarter, the bloodied black man would much rather lash out in anger at the referee for his ignorance, silence, or willful head turning than lash out at the other players who have been inflicting the pain.

Continuing and concluding with the "referee" illustration, I am going to step out and say that many blacks see many whites and white institutions, such as the government and the church, as the "ref." For some reason, I have a burden to educate and embrace the "ref," while many others have the desire to beat up the "ref." There are a growing number of black people like myself who desire to relate to the "ref." But sadly so, there are also many blacks that have thrown in the towel and have said, "to heck with it; forget the 'ref'; let's bandage ourselves, comfort ourselves, care for ourselves, and cause ourselves to grow." Thus you have black organizations, magazines, TV, corporations, social clubs, etc.

We begin to minister to ourselves—but then the straw that breaks the camel's angry back, is when the "ref" comes over to the black team's bench and says, "Why do you need these organizations, magazines, etc.? Let's just all be a team. Let's just all get along. Let's all just be Americans!"

DA

David,

First a clarification: I think you misunderstood my comments about the publishing of the article in Jet magazine. I certainly would not deny anyone the right to publish their own special-interest magazine nor to print articles such as these. Jet focuses in on a target market and I'm sure it serves that market well. I was questioning the effectiveness of publishing the article in Jet, if the intent of the article is to help eliminate racism in America.

You mentioned in your letter that you were shocked by my comments about the article. Disappointment and frustration also came through in your words. Our letters have revealed a couple things to me: (1) that this racial reconciliation thing is a metamorphosis or evolutionary process that cannot occur overnight nor even over a short period of time; and (2) that the transformation that occurs in the person who pursues this reconciliation is not unlike the changes that occur during the discipleship process of a new believer.

We know that once a sinner becomes a new believer they need to be discipled to nurture their growth and to help them fully understand the truths of the Scriptures. To the lifelong believer the ignorance of the new convert can be overwhelming, their thought processes shocking, and their actions or words often disturbing—but as the new believer matures, their ignorance is replaced by knowledge, their thought processes regenerated, and their actions and words become more Christ-like. To watch a new believer grow to spiritual maturity is truly wonderful. However, one of the great dangers when a person embraces Christianity is that they turn back to their old ways, beliefs, and lifestyles having rejected the "conversion" as a phase they went through.

When it comes to spiritual giftedness and approaches to evangelism, you and I are very different. You have a strong vein of the evangelist in you, but I am more the shepherd than evangelist. You desire to lead anyone and everyone to Christ no matter where you are or if you will ever see them again to be able to follow up with them. I, on the other hand, shy away from "evangelizing" someone unless I myself can follow up with them to help ensure their growth or unless I know specifically that someone else will be watching out for them. What is important about this, as it relates to racial reconciliation, is that we each approach the matter of reconciliation the same way we approach evangelism of the gospel.

You stated in your letter that you have a burden to educate, embrace, and relate to whites—i.e., evangelize racial reconciliation through relationship. This is important and I am glad that there are more and more African Americans like yourself who are directly "evangelizing" whites about racism and reconciliation through relationship. However, what I'm missing is that I see no shepherds to do the "discipleship" that seems to be necessary to complete the process of reconciliation in the "evangelized converts."

The schism between our races has been so large for so long that there are now so many different facets and issues to racial reconciliation in this country that without such "discipleship" I believe all efforts toward reconciliation by a thousand "evangelists" will be in vain.

I know that treating all persons without bias or discrimination is such a simple concept that you may feel I am blowing this to extreme proportions. However, living life like Christ would live life and putting our full trust in His provision is also a simple concept. Yet I know from personal experience that applying simple biblical concepts to our everyday world is not always so easy to do.

I have been "evangelized" about racism in America; I believe it exists and that there needs to be massive reconciliation between our races. I want to run a good race; I want to cross the finish line of reconciliation, and then turn around and help others. But I cannot take this journey alone, without a guide. I realize that I am asking an extremely busy evangelist to also be a shepherd, but if you don't, who will? I know no other "guides."

Do not be surprised, my friend, that my response to the article about the teens fit into the typical white response about racism. After three years of day-in and day-out discipleship by Jesus, in the garden before the crucifixion, Peter cut off the ear of a Roman soldier. Hardly the response you would expect from the "Rock" on whom the church would be built.

One last clarification: "The trap of disbelief and pity," my words were that "I did not want to believe," not that "I did not believe." The former is "disbelief"; the latter is, at least for me, coming to terms with a fact that I had previously thought or hoped was not true.

Perhaps I was previously entangled in the "trap of disbelief" but now I am struggling with the acknowledgment that it is people like me who keep the coals of racism burning. The implications of this knock the wind out of me because they mean that I may be guilty and part of the problem, and that my friends and family may be guilty and part of the problem. The implications are that my grandparents and my wife's grandparents who were adults during the days of Jim Crow segregation were part of the problem because they went along with the segregation. The implications are that my parents who were starting their family during the civil rights era were part of the problem because they attended a Christian college, and later sent my sister to the same college, that today still holds to racist beliefs.*

*Sometime after this letter was written the university changed its policies, which were in my opinion racist policies. Defenders of the university claim that their policies were never racist but that they were based on biblical principles. I do not doubt the sincerity of the university's belief in their doctrine; however, I believe their doctrine (in this one specific area) to be inconsistent with Christ's teachings that regardless of our racial origin we are all part of His family and there should no longer be racial separation.

The implication is that when in the past I or my friends and family have spoken disparagingly about "blacks" as a racial group that I was part of the problem.

I want to believe that the problems are somebody else's fault, that they are the sins of the past not the present. I want to believe . . . does not mean any longer that I do believe . . . it means I see the facts and am coming to the realization that they are the truth, not what I previously believed.

BZ

Brent,

Thank you for your honesty. Most of all thank you for your humility. I am somewhat humbled by your response because it shows that I have a lot of room to grow in the way I communicate. It also demonstrates that, regarding these issues of race, I still have in my heart seeds of anger that I thought were nonexistent. In addition, your response shows me that my role cannot be just the evangelist but the discipler as well. Yes, I will help walk with you through this journey of reconciliation while simultaneously learning, stretching, and growing myself.

Thank you for helping me be a better discipler.

DA

Where am I on the continuum of racial reconciliation?

We see racial reconciliation in the United States not as something that is a onetime achievement in a person's life attained by completing certain tasks or assignments, but rather as a continuum along which we must continually progress or digress. This question was a pause in the dialogue for Brent to inquire of David, "How am I doing with this racial reconciliation thing?" Based on what you have read so far, what do you think David's answer will be?

David,

*W*here do I currently stand on the continuum of racial reconciliation? Does a person's skin color matter to me?

If you had asked me this question when we started our letter writing I would have answered quickly, confidently, and proudly: "No, the color of a person's skin does not matter to me at all," a response I think you would consistently find if you asked the same question to most whites who do not openly subscribe to white-supremacist or hate-group ideology. My answer today however has changed. Today my answer would be the same answer given by Klansmen or Nazis. Today I would say: "Yes, the color of a person's skin does matter and it matters so much it affects every encounter

I have with a person of another race." Lest you worry that I have digressed and embraced racist ideology, let me assure you that my reasons for answering the way I did are entirely different than the reasons a hate group or white supremacist group would have. The reason the color of a person's skin matters to me isn't because I'm superior, they're inferior, or because I resent, despise, or hate a person of another color.

The reason the color of skin matters is simply that we do not live in a color-blind world. The color of your skin will often open or close doors to experiences and situations that will differ from experiences or situations that I will encounter in life. Other people with your color of skin will most likely face similar experiences and situations that you do. Knowing this I can be relatively confident that it would be inappropriate for me to give you a Confederate flag to fly outside your house. My internal acknowledgment that you do not "come to the table" of our relationship with the same background of experiential influences that I do keeps me from trying to fit you into the box of my own "experiential influences." This allows our friendship the opportunity to be dynamic.

Where do I stand on the continuum of racial reconciliation? Based on what you have told me, the perception of at least one member of Bridgeway's board of trustees is that I have reconciled with blacks like you, but that I still have a problem with blacks from "the 'hood." Is this perception correct? The simple answer is yes, 100 percent correct. The reality of it all is that I probably stand in the same general vicinity along the continuum that the majority of whites who attend Bridgeway stand. I am reconciled to those whom I call friend and to those who I believe hold no animosity or ill will toward me. The important question, though, is why do I stand where I stand? Why am I not further along the continuum toward reconciliation? Am I a closet racist? Am I a person who makes exceptions for certain individuals but holds disdain for the race as a whole?

I have conceded that I am reconciled to certain individuals but unreconciled to the entire race. But why? And what am I doing about it? Is it possible to be reconciled to all persons of a given race? As a Christian we are called to love all persons, not just those who love us, like us, or look similar to us. We may not be able to be individually reconciled to all persons of another race but it seems to me that we must at least be reconciled to the particular racial group. You see, DA, this is what makes our letters so crucial. I may be reconciled to you but if I'm not reconciled to the group known as African Americans, I haven't crossed the finish line. I want to run a good race; I want to cross the finish line; I want to obey the command to *love* people that may be a challenge for me to love. To do this I can't just say a prayer, wave a wand, and declare that "O.K., I now love all people." There are difficult issues that need to be resolved, or at least addressed.

I have a problem with blacks from "the 'hood." Is it because their skin is black? Or is it because of the lifestyle and subculture that they choose to embrace? For me this is a vital question and I must answer with all possible honesty lest I deceive myself. However, this is also a vital question for you. You know my concession. Now what do you do with that information? Do you and me (who heretofore were reconciled) now have "a problem" because I am unreconciled to all blacks? Does my concession leave you guarded so that you keep me at a distance?

I get the impression that most blacks will do just that until they feel that I am reconciled to the entire racial group. This response is the natural response to being unable to answer the "Why am I not yet reconciled" question about someone else. If the answer to such a question about me is, Because their skin is black, then the sin of racism must be dealt with in my soul before reconciliation can proceed. If the answer to the question is, lifestyle and culture, then reconciliation can continue. I would venture however that many are not able to confidently answer the "why" question about others—either because they do not know the person adequately to know their heart or because they lack the ability to rightly discern the truth about themselves or others.

Here is the question then for you: Why am I unreconciled to/with blacks from "the 'hood"? I feel confident with how I would answer but I am curious as to how you perceive the situation.

BZ

Brent,

*Y*ou know yourself well and you are honest enough to verbalize what you truly feel. We all have prejudices that we need to grow out of. This happens through relational and cultural experiences. As you walk with me and I walk with you, I believe that you will begin to have an integrated mindset that sees the "boys in the hood" as a different culture. It is a culture that you don't have to like, but at minimum, appreciate. There are negative things that you don't have to appreciate about another person's culture. I know that there are aspects of many different cultures that I do not like. There are aspects of my own culture that I don't like. However, it is important that we understand cultural differences and identify them as such.

Some of these differences from the "hood" are music, dress, terminology, and style. There is no reason for you to "disdain," as you put it, people who are different from you. They are not better or worse than you, just different. People may have different values, attitudes, opinions, and habits than you do as a middle-class white man. That's okay though! As a Christian, you do not have the right to look down on anyone who is different than you because all people matter to God.

And let's not associate evil things and criminal activities with culture. Why? Because no one wins. You will say blacks from the hood commit a set of criminal acts and I will say whites commit another set of criminal acts. This isn't right. Environment, upbringing, class distinctions, and circumstances all play a role in criminal activity. Criminal activity is not inherited by any one culture. Given the same variables, any race could and would commit the same crimes. This is not a skin problem but a sin problem. My guess is that you have a problem with people from the hood because you don't feel safe and you don't like the same things those from the hood like. Well, guess what, I am the same way. Although I can appreciate some things from the hood, I don't always feel safe or value the same things as they might. Why? Because our classes are different. Class is oftentimes an issue that distinguishes people's likes and dislikes. If my assessment is correct about why you have problems with people in the hood, you may then ask, "What's the difference between our views regarding the hood?" Here's the difference: As a black man I still feel emotionally connected to, responsible for, and feel compassion for those in the hood because they are my people. I feel concerned and a sense of compassion for those who are downtrodden and caught in a web of disrepute. My guess is that you don't feel this way about those in the city. I don't think that your heart beats to be an agent of change through prayer and service to those black folks in the hood. I believe that you would probably view them as irresponsible and criminal people who sulk in a victim mentality. I could be wrong and please correct me if I am. That's the difference. The difference is not our status but our perspective.

You asked me to identify where you are on the continuum. If the far left of the continuum was a stone-cold racist and the far right extreme was a fully reconciled ambassador of racial reconciliation, I would place you just to the right of the halfway point. Why? Because the halfway point is someone who has a growing relationship with someone with whom they can candidly discuss issues of race for the purpose of understanding. I see you doing this. I like the fact that you are not completely satisfied with where you are, but at least you are trying to understand.

DA

Who should apologize?

The next two sections of letters deal with repentance, forgiveness, and the appropriateness of whites extending an apology to blacks for past injustices. In other words it gets down to two questions: Who is to blame? and Who has to take the heat? As you would expect, blacks and whites have very differing opinions on this. What you might not expect, though, is that whites are not in complete agreement—even whites who agree that an apology should be extended.

David,

O.K., buddy, here we go: to apologize or not?—a question that truly I still have and still struggle with.

A significant contention of African Americans is that there has never been repentance by whites for the centuries of atrocities committed against blacks. These atrocities include but are not limited to slavery; crimes committed against slaves, such as murder, assault, and rape; segregation; violent intimidation; verbal and mental oppression; and discrimination. Whites typically want to leave the past in the past and to go forward on "a level playing field," viewing repentance or an apology as unnecessary if not inappropriate. Blacks typically contend that, even though slavery was abolished, civil rights laws enacted, discrimination outlawed, and affirmative action established, there has been no repentance. Therefore whites cannot be trusted, have not truly turned from their racist ways, and continue to discreetly discriminate and promote racist ideology.

As I understand the word and the concept, repentance has three components: (1) an admission of wrong, (2) a request for forgiveness, and (3) a change in behavior on a go-forward basis to no longer commit the wrong. From a macroanalysis, components 1 and 3 have been embraced or at least acknowledged by whites in abolishing slavery, enacting civil rights legislation, outlawing discrimination, and establishing affirmative action programs. However, at the same macrolevel, up until recently, there have been few or no apologies requesting forgiveness—component 2 has been omitted.

Without an apology whites have never had to personally accept blame for the wrongs. The "wrongdoings" have been kept at a comfortable distance and only acknowledged as being wrong, but it was someone else's fault. Without an apology blacks have never felt they could trust whites. They remain suspicious that whites have not truly turned from their racist ways and are only giving lip service to an expedient answer to social and political problems.

Clearly a post–Civil War or post–civil rights apology should have been extended, but it wasn't, and that was then and this is now, and we are left with the question of do we apologize today for the wrongs of a generation or century ago? To answer this question I think we need to go back to the basics of repentance and ask the question of who should repent for a wrong committed? To me the obvious answer is the person, entity, or institution that committed the wrong.

There is another answer promoted, though, that is not so obvious and it is an answer that I struggle with as to whether it is correct. The second answer says that not only is the person who committed the wrong guilty, but that any person who benefited from the commission of the wrong is guilty also and should therefore repent of the original offense. The problem with this theory, though, is how do you define "benefit"? Do you look at this at a microlevel or a macrolevel?

Microanalysis would say that the grandchildren who have inherited the financial wealth of their slave owner ancestors, whose wealth was built on the backs of slaves, would have reason to repent. When this same cause of repentance is translated to a macroanalysis, it requires that all whites repent even if they have no connection to the slave owner other than being of the same race; it is at this intangible benefit level that I have a problem with the concept.

For the time being at least, let's not debate the "intangible benefit" and let's go back to the "obvious answer" since I think we can cover a lot of ground here. On June 20, 1995, the Southern Baptist Convention humbled itself and passed a resolution repenting of the denomination's racist history. The resolution passed by the convention repenting of racism surprised me because I had no idea that the denomination was created because of a split between the North and the South over slavery and whether slave owners could be missionaries. Nor did I know that the denomination was silent or actively opposed to the civil rights movement through the 1970s.

As I understand the resolution from the newspaper articles I've read, not only did the denomination as an institution repent but it asked its members to, where appropriate, apologize and repent also.* A couple things stood out to me about this. The institution apologized; the correct "who" that should have apologized did. The convention in the resolution also asked the denomination's members who have committed similar wrongs to repent and apologize too. What would these similar wrongs be? Since no one currently living ever owned a slave, presumably the wrongs could be: discrimination, a desire for and/or promotion of segregation, silence in the face of injustices committed against blacks, active opposition to the expansion of the civil rights of a racial minority group, and even simple disparaging words or thoughts about the African American, black, colored, Negro race.

*See the articles in appendix B.

I found the words of the minister who helped draft the convention's resolution very liberating and challenging as to who should repent. "Certainly we do not ask anyone to join in confessing wrongs of which you are not guilty." This statement is liberating to me as a white person because it tells me I do not have to feel guilty or apologize or repent for wrongs I did not commit. At the same time this statement challenges me to examine myself and to apologize and repent for the wrongs I am guilty of. It challenges me to examine my heart to determine if I am guilty of either sins of "commission" or "omission." One of the Southern Baptist denomination's sins of "commission" was to condone slavery. One of the sins of "omission" was to remain silent and do nothing to right obvious wrongs. James 4:17 pierces directly to the heart of these sins of omission. "Therefore, to him who knows to do good and does not do it, to him it is sin" (NKJV).

The topic of whites' apologizing to African Americans for the atrocities of the past is getting increased attention these days. Raleigh Washington and Glen Kehrein spend a fair amount of time discussing the subject in their book "Breaking Down Walls," and Promise Keepers has made it a major point in their conferences. The impression I got from reading Washington and Kehrein was that if you're white, you're guilty of all the atrocities past and present and you should repent for your racist history. They go as far as to say that whites individually are obliged to seek forgiveness for the racism of the group, and they use the Old Testament prophets to substantiate this claim.

> Most of us understand the need for repentance for sins we personally commit against another. But many of us struggle with the concept of taking responsibility for the sins of the group of which we are a part—whether that is our family, our nation, our race, or our ethnic group—especially when we feel personally innocent. But we are responsible for such sins, the Bible teaches (page 199).

The writers then reference Daniel 9:15–16; Ezra 9:6–7; Nehemiah 1:6–7; and Exodus 32:31–32 using these verses and leaders as examples of individuals accepting responsibility for the sins of the group even though they personally were not guilty of the sin they were confessing.

> Notice that none of these leaders was personally guilty of the sin for which he was repenting. Yet each took responsibility for the corporate sin, accepting it as his own. Reconciliation grew out of their godly prayers of repentance. Similarly you and I must accept responsibility for the sins of our group, and then take whatever action is necessary to bring about reconciliation (page 200).

I agree that each of the leaders was not personally guilty of the sin for which they were repenting. I agree that they were repenting to God for the corporate sins of the nation. I disagree as to why they were repenting. Washington and Kehrein imply that the leader's repentance was an example: that each of us individually should repent and ask forgiveness (presumably from both God and man) for wrongs committed by someone else, a group of someone else's, or a nation of which we are one individual. I think there are two important distinctions between the leaders mentioned and Joe average white man on the street.

First, these men were the leaders of the Israelite people. And it was in their "leader" capacity that they were requesting forgiveness from God. This is similar to the leadership of the Southern Baptist convention requesting forgiveness for the racist sins of the denomination. They were not individually assuming responsibility and blame for all the sins of the institution and its members; they were, in their leadership capacity, repenting and requesting forgiveness for the sins of the institution. Comparable to Moses requesting forgiveness for the sins of the Israelites for building the golden calf isn't Brent Zuercher requesting forgiveness for the centuries of racist atrocities committed by this nation; comparable would be President Bill Clinton requesting forgiveness. Moses was the leader of the Israelites, and Bill Clinton is the leader of this nation—that is comparable.

Secondly, in the days of the Old Testament an individual received forgiveness of his sins by offering a sacrifice such as an unblemished lamb. People took their lambs to the temple to offer as a sacrifice. Once a year, if I'm remembering correctly, the Jewish high priest would enter the Holy of Holies and would offer the sacrifice of the people to God in seeking forgiveness for their sins. It wasn't until the death and resurrection of Jesus that God changed the rules of forgiveness. There is no longer a need for a high priest to intercede on our behalf or on behalf of our nation. With the cross we all individually became priests, gained access to God, and no longer are we one person requesting and receiving forgiveness for the sins of the group as a whole.

You passed on to me a cassette tape of a sermon by a white pastor friend of yours in the Columbia area on the topic of white apologies to blacks. I've listened to the tape and again I find myself in the uncomfortable position of disagreeing with a minister. Your friend's assertion is that 1 Samuel 15 and Zephaniah 2:8–11, documenting God's instructions to the Israelites to attack and annihilate the Amalekites and Ammonites (two nations who had committed atrocities against the Israelites centuries earlier), are evidence that in God's eyes the descendant is guilty of the ancestor's sin; therefore the descendant should repent of the sins of the ancestor. Your friend contends that Adam's introduction of sin into mankind, thereby giving us our sinful nature, is also proof that in God's eyes the descendant is guilty of the sin of the ancestor. I do not contest that through Adam man inherited a sinful nature but I do contest that I am guilty of the sins of my known ancestors back to the 1500s and the unknown prior to that. I can guarantee that I have not repented of enough sins if I must repent for the sum total of all my ancestors' sins since Adam.

Rather than evidencing that God views the descendant guilty of the sins of the ancestor, I believe the passages evidence God's justice in God's own timing. The Israelites were victims of atrocities committed against them by both the

Amalekites and the Ammonites. Vengeance is the Lord's, and in His timing, and that very well may mean that the victim will never see justice done in their lifetime. In the case of the Ammonites, God's vengeance and justice came 700 years after the commission of the injustice. Were the descendants guilty of the ancestor's sin? Or were the consequences of the ancestor's sin visited on the descendants? I propose the latter.

We both know that every sin has consequences that are irreversible even if the sin is confessed and forgiven. For example, a convicted mass murderer on death row may find salvation of his soul and spend eternity in heaven yet he still must face the executioner as a consequence of his sins. In the text of the Ten Commandments we are told that the sins of the father are visited on his children to the third and fourth generation. Although I do not agree that all whites are guilty of past atrocities committed by others, I am fully persuaded that the consequences of the sins of our ancestors and their peers may be visited on me personally or on my descendants. I do not think America has yet begun to fully feel the consequences of the sins of slavery, segregation, discrimination, or racism that have not been repented for over the years, decades, and centuries.

I think your pastor friend made a good point for reconciliation, though, when he referenced 2 Samuel 21. Israel was suffering through a famine as a consequence of King Saul's previous disobedience to God in dealing with the Gibeonites. King David did the wise thing and went to the Gibeonites to reconcile with them so that God would lessen His judgment on the Israelites. Saul's disobedience had consequences for the entire Israelite nation, years after his death. The implication here is that likewise whites should approach African Americans seeking reconciliation so that not only will God lessen His judgment on us but that we come into obedience by loving our brothers as ourselves.

There is one other problem that I have with the arguments that say whites today should apologize for the sins of prior generations and that whites should acknowledge and assume the responsibility for the atrocities committed by our race's ancestors. My problem is that these calls for assumption of responsibility, repentance, and apologies are an easy out. I disagree theologically that I am guilty of someone else's sin. But if I were to be persuaded that such theology is correct; to accept the blame for the sins of the past and to apologize for them is the easy way out that I believe doesn't address the heart of the racism problem today.

It is much easier for me to "take the fall" for someone else's wrong than it is to admit my own wrong. If I take the heat for someone else I get to feel good about myself. Seeing someone else's failure on a larger scale helps me to feel good about myself because my failure might not be quite so grand. If I focus in on slavery and Jim Crow segregation, I'm inclined by comparison to discount by own contributions to racism and racial disunity. If I focus on apologizing for past atrocities of which I had no part, I have less ability to focus on my own heart and to test it, purge it, repent of the contribution I have made, and work to help restore unity between our races.

In closing, I commit to you that I will take the time in the next few weeks to search my heart and ask God to heighten my conscience to understand how I personally have sinned and contributed to racism and racial disunity. I also commit that I will repent of my sin, and that I will do what I can to help restore unity between myself and my African American brothers and sisters. I ask you to do this for me, that as quickly as possible you write back to me about your perspective, insights, and thoughts about this topic of apologies by whites. Am I close to the truth? Or in the words of your pastor friend, "Am I just fooling myself?"

BZ

Brent,

To apologize or not to apologize? That's the question on the table. Who is guilty and who does God hold responsible for the atrocities of the white man on the black man?

You believe that all whites cannot be held personally responsible for racism but need to repent where appropriate. My response is based on the following four passages: Romans 3:23; Matthew 5:23–24; Matthew 18:15; and 1 Peter 2:9, and can be summed up as simply: We are all guilty. We are all responsible. We will all pay!

Romans 3:23 says that we have all "sinned and fall short of the glory of God." In other words, white people had the guns and the power and they did what evil men do. They sinned. The bottom line is simple; we are all depraved. If blacks had had the money, guns, and power, we might have done the same thing given the opportunity. What white folk did to black folk was heinous and evil. There will be consequences for such behavior for many centuries to come. I agree with you when you said, "I do not think America has yet begun to fully feel the consequences of the sins of slavery, segregation, discrimination, or racism that have not been repented for over the years, decades, and centuries." Sinners sin and the effects of heinous sin produces chilling repercussions.

Should whites apologize? Of course. You'd better believe it. But the real question is which whites? And the grander question is to whom? Matthew 5:23–24 helps answer this. Jesus tells me that if I sense that my brother has a problem with me that it is my responsibility to go to my brother and resolve our differences. Guess what? Your black brothers have a problem with you. Therefore it is the responsibility of Christian white men to seek racial reconciliation with their black brothers. This also means that it is Christian white men who have the burden of repentance. True reconciliation will not come through our government, nor should we expect it to. The church must lead the charge regarding repentance and reconciliation.

The other side of the coin is found in Matthew 18 where Jesus tells me that if my brother has sinned against me that I must go to him to work through issues of reconciliation. This is the job of the black man. The black Christian must be willing to forgive and apologize for his sin born out of bitterness.

This apologetic spirit and forgiving spirit don't come from counting every sin committed because we cannot number them. For example, in a marriage it is difficult for a couple in counseling to recall all of the mean things said and the bad decisions made out of anger. Usually the couple on the brink of divorce has hurt each other so deeply that it will take a spirit of brokenness, repentance, and forgiveness to wash away the laundry list of transgression.

We as Christian brothers cannot argue about who should apologize and who should not. The list is too long. We are all too guilty of making some contribution to the deep wounds that plague us. The issues are too complex to determine that all whites are guilty and under divine judgment. The issues are too intertwined to determine personal innocence.

The issue of the apology is not about whether I say, "I am sorry" or not. It is about whether I am a Christian or not. If I am a Christian, then I am more than sorry, I am sick. I am sick to see sin and its consequences rear their ugly head.

As a Christian, I am to have a reconciling spirit, a spirit that says, like an abused wife in a bad marriage would say, "I don't deserve this, I am not responsible for the sins of my husband, nor will I take on the shame of his sin, but I can own up to what I've done wrong in this process." Such an attitude is the beginning of the healing process for the wife. Likewise, the battering husband bears a lot of the blame and he must own up to his sin. He must repent and feel the depth of his transgressions against his wife. He must change his behavior and seek forgiveness and healing from his wife.

So then, what about the white man's apology? Allow me to carry the battered wife illustration a little further. If you are the brother of a battering husband, are you guilty by association? You look alike. You have the same last name. Yet, although you didn't hit the woman, you sense her anger towards you as well. Just like the sister of the battered wife might feel the pain of her sister by family association, the brother of the husband might feel the guilt of his brother by family association. I think the brother of the battering husband could have had an indirect part in the abuse. I do not know the history of the husband and brother's relationship or family upbringing, but it is conceivable that the brother could have contributed to the family problem. Who knows? Most likely, the brother had nothing to do with any of this. However, most importantly, the brother must minister comfort to the battered wife because there is some guilt by association. Think about it. Most family feuds are carried on by those who carry a certain last name. In this race war (so to speak), our color is our dividing line. Someone must take the lead and lift up the white flag of surrender.

Regarding an apology, I am going to suggest that the job is ours! Whose? Ours! Christians'! First Peter 2:9 says that we are all priests. It is my job as a believer and your job as a believer to confess and repent for ourselves and our people. I should be so sick over the sins of myself and my people that I am willing to apologize, repent, intercede for, and forgive anyone and everyone. I am sure we are all guilty of contributing to this problem. We cannot move forward until we realize this point.

I am not expecting or demanding that all whites apologize for the sins of their forefathers. It would be nice if our government did this on a large scale, but I'm not holding my breath. However, my expectations of white Christians is that they have an apologetic spirit for any way they may have caused, benefited from, or been a part of such a criminal heritage, either by direct contact or by association.

Will any of us ever know what percentage of blame we bear in the historical atrocities of the past? Of course not. But we all agree that we have somehow, some way, incurred some guilt in this process. An apologetic spirit and a forgiving spirit are the prerequisites to seeing clearly the specifics of my sin.

This approach to the "apology" issue is the one I believe God will honor most. I believe that Christians who embrace this approach to reconciliation will come much closer to the heart of God than any other I know.

DA

When should we forgive?

David,

Repentance or forgiveness, which comes first? You alluded to this in your last letter and I'd like to discuss it further. Conventional biblical wisdom is that a person cannot be forgiven if they haven't repented. We know that for a person to receive the salvation of their soul they must admit their sinful nature and confess their sin to God (repentance precedes forgiveness). We also know that when a spouse commits infidelity, they must repent of their sin to both God and their spouse (repentance precedes forgiveness). In almost every example you look at, repentance precedes forgiveness, forgiveness precedes reconciliation, and therefore repentance precedes reconciliation.

This is true for almost every biblical example because Christ had to give us sinful offenders many examples so that it would get through our thick skulls that as offenders, we desperately need to repent of our offenses before God and receive His forgiveness. However, I am left with a nagging question of whether this conventional wisdom applies to both the offender and the victim. Certainly an offender cannot receive forgiveness until they have repented of their offense. But does this mean that the victim does not have to forgive until an apology is extended?

We know that in the context of racial reconciliation that the offender's appropriate perspective and response is one of humility and repentance. But what is the victim's appropriate perspective and response? I would suggest that when a victim views forgiveness from the perspective of the offender, that the victim is not responding as God desires victims to respond.

I propose that the victim's perspective should be that forgiveness can and should precede the extension of an apology by the offender. Why? Two reasons. First, because Christ demonstrated this principle on the cross when He said, "Father, forgive them; for they know not what they do" (Luke 23:34 KJV). Jesus Himself forgave His offenders before any repentance was offered. At the cross Christ assumed all past and future sins and at that point in time God the Father forgave us of our sins, even those of us living today. God (the victim) initiated reconciliation with sinful man (the offender). How is reconciliation with God completed? By the offender repenting and accepting God's forgiveness. God's forgiveness is a gift we are not worthy of and which we must merely accept. Even when a sinner as evil as a serial murderer repents today of his sins, there is no new act of forgiveness that God must perform. It was all settled at the cross.

Secondly, in Mark 11:25–26 (NKJV) Christ states, "If you have anything against anyone, forgive him, that your Father in heaven may also forgive your trespasses. But if you do not forgive, neither will your Father in heaven forgive your trespasses." This is the other side of the coin to Matthew 5:23, which states that if anyone has anything against us, that it must be our priority to be reconciled with the person offended by us. When we comprehend our own sinful wickedness and the wholly undeserved mercy and grace that God extends to us, then we cannot help but forgive those who have wronged us like we have wronged God. It is not possible for us to repent of our wrongs and to also hold on to an unforgiving spirit toward those who have wronged us.

My friend, in these last two paragraphs I have dared to tread into doctrinal statements when I have neither the education nor training to do so. But to me, a layman, it appears that just as we are all guilty of contributing to the problem and therefore personally responsible to examine our hearts, to repent, apologize, and seek reconciliation, we are all also personally responsible to forgive those who have committed an offense against us—even if the offender never apologizes.

When I first thought about the forgiveness issue, I thought practically it only applied to African Americans, that I, with other whites, needed to focus on repentance, and that blacks needed to focus on forgiveness. However, as I look at the concept of forgiveness I tend to think that blacks and whites need to focus on both repentance and forgiveness. I must repent for those offenses that I have committed and I must forgive those offenses that I have been the recipient of—even if the offender never repents. I cannot harbor resentment in my heart towards someone who I believe has offended or wronged me. This is a difficult task; how do I do this? How do you forgive an unrepentant offender? What are your insights on this? Is this a step we must take? Or can we all just wait around for an apology?

BZ

Brent,

You asked about forgiveness. In fact you stated: "How do you forgive an unrepentant offender? What are your insights on this? Is this a step we must take? Or can we all just wait around for an apology?"

I agree with you regarding forgiveness and repentance. God has called us to reconciliation. This goes beyond tolerance and respect. This is a core value of Christians. In 2 Corinthians 5, Christ-followers are called "Christ's ambassadors." There is a difference between forgiveness and reconciliation. Although I can forgive an unrepentant offender,

I may not be able to reconcile with that offender until repentance takes place. Repentance is indeed the bridge between forgiveness and reconciliation.

Colossians 3:13 says: "Bear with each other and forgive whatever grievances you may have against one another. Forgive as the Lord forgave you" (NIV). God desires you and me to forgive each other's grievances. I may have grievances against you that I may need to forgive; however, reconciliation will not be possible until the grievances are resolved. For instance, a battered wife can forgive her abusive husband, but I would counsel that woman that she cannot be reconciled until his behavior changes and he goes through counseling. So then, can you forgive someone like Louis Farrakhan whom I know you are offended by? Sure. When you forgive him, are you then reconciled with him? No. Do you need to be? I don't think so. Why? Because there is no relationship. Your job is to love him and pray for him. However, if you have an issue in your heart against him, then forgiveness may be necessary. Only God can clarify that one for you, so I encourage you to go to Him for direction.

Brent, I often tell black folks not to wait for an apology from white folks before you love them and forgive them because God has called us to love and forgive in spite of what someone has done to offend us. This cannot be seen as a way to avert conflict, however. We are called to go to our offender and speak the truth in love as we inform him of his sin against God and us. This is easier said than done, of course. But we must do it if we are going to reconcile. But just remember, sinners sin! That's what they do best. I have never expected to witness reconciliation in the world because it is a theological term. True reconciliation can only take place in the church. I can only love the sinner and point him toward the God he must reconcile with first.

But within the church, I have brothers and sisters of all different shapes and shades, and it is my responsibility to pursue peace and reconciliation for the sake of unity. You see, forgiveness is not just an act but a process. Often it takes time for one's heart to emotionally catch up with one's mental and spiritual decision to forgive. Forgiveness is an issue of obedience as well. Therefore, it is imperative to walk in truth and obedience no matter how you feel. I heard Dr. Stowell, president of Moody Bible Institute, once say, "Obedience is not always easy, but it is always right!"

DA

Reconciliation begins

We have come to the final series of letters we exchanged on this topic of racial reconciliation. This series of letters is not about a specific question or issue under the umbrella of racial reconciliation. These letters are the natural result of an honest inspection of our own heart and mind and life. All letters to this point were merely the prelude to the beginning of reconciliation. When a person accepts Jesus Christ as his or her Lord and Savior, it may be the conclusion of a search for spiritual truth regarding salvation, but it is the beginning of new life as a child of God for eternity. Similarly the conclusion of the search for truth on racial matters is only the beginning of true racial reconciliation.

David,

*I*magine with me (if you can) just generally not being liked by five out of six people you meet. Imagine knowing that five out of six people would prefer not to interact with you because they don't like the way you look, walk, talk, drive, or clothe yourself. Imagine how many job interviews you would have to go on to actually be hired instead of being passed over because five out of six interviewers generally just don't get a comfortable feel about you, or don't think you'd mesh well with "the team." Imagine being a law-abiding citizen living in a town that doesn't have a lot of crime, but every time a crime is committed, the entire town assumes you or one of your family members committed the crime because your uncle's cousin by a second marriage was convicted of a crime in the next county. Imagine finally scraping enough money together to make a down payment on a small but comfortable house, qualifying for the loan, diligently searching for a "dream house" that doesn't bury you in debt—and then every time you find a house you like, five out of the six neighbors want nothing to do with you and would prefer that you not move in. Imagine being nine years old and realizing that for the rest of your life, while probably not being in danger of physical harm, five out of six people will not give you the benefit of the doubt, will begin interacting with you not because they want to but because they have to, and generally prefer that you keep out of their life.

What a world that would be! I think I would hate it! I think I would resent those five out of six people, and I think if given the choice I would choose a different world to live in. I can hardly imagine the difficulty of living in such an environment. Can you?

Unfortunately it's probably not that hard for you to imagine because I think African Americans live in just such a world in our country. Who and what created such an environment for you to live in? Was it slave masters wielding a whip? emotionally charged segregationists? minority-hating white supremacists who advocate an ethnic cleansing of sorts? Unfortunately I don't think so. I think the people who created such an unfriendly place for blacks to live in were people like me: nonviolent, churchgoing, family people. In fact I think I helped create just such a place, maybe not in your neighborhood, but in my own. You see I created in my mind certain stereotypes about blacks and I let these stereotypes permeate my thoughts, my words, my heart, and my relationships. I generally just didn't like black people and I preferred that my life not interact with too many on a personal level. Oh, I could have black friends—I didn't have any until college, but in college and postcollege I have had black friends. Of course these friends, like yourself, had to almost be directly opposite the stereotype I had defined all other blacks with.

What was my stereotype?

The first component that jumps to mind was that blacks are a violent people. I felt that although they may appear civil and friendly on the outside, if you accidentally hit their hot button, your life and possessions may very well be in danger. What did I base such a conclusion on?—the Los Angeles riots including the beating of Reginald Denny who happened to be in the wrong place at the wrong time, the prevalence of gangs and gang-related violence in black communities, gangsta rap, and the observation that when African American families move to suburban homes away from the mayhem of the inner city, violence and gangs follow them and impact previously peaceful communities.

Secondly, I felt that blacks were a people filled with and consumed by hate and bitterness. This conclusion was driven by Nation of Islam rhetoric, again some of the lyrics of rap music, and once again the South Central Los Angeles riots.

I felt that blacks had an amazing and illogical draw toward self-destruction as evidenced by riots and drugs.

I felt they were lazy and were slobs. They walked slow, drove slow, lived on welfare, and left their neighborhoods trash-strewn, run-down dumps.

I was convinced that almost all blacks were whiners and complainers whose favorite maneuver was to "play the race card" against whites.

However, by far my most comprehensive stereotype was that blacks were irresponsible. After all, who else lived off welfare indefinitely without attempting to support themselves or their family? Who else had a staggering rate of teenage pregnancy? Which other race had such a high occurrence of single parents where the biological father was either unknown or absent from the child's life? Which other race blamed another race for all the problems and hurdles and embarrassments they experienced? And who else spent money needed to provide for basic family necessities on drugs or expensive high-top basketball shoes?

In my mind I had taken the above fragments of experience and observation and had created a stereotype by which I not only defined a subgroup or individuals of a race, but by which I defined an entire race.

As I read over this stereotype of mine again, I imagine myself sharing such a confession to Joe average white man on the street. I see this person, who has just heard my stereotype, look at me, shrug his shoulders, and say "So what?" And, in part, this person would be right. I never beat anyone, burned a cross on their lawn, or threatened anyone. I never denied anyone employment because of their race and I never shouted racial slurs at anyone. All I did was form some opinions based on observation and I created a stereotype with which I defined a race—no blood, no foul.

But just as this person would be right, they are also wrong. If I was alone in my stereotype, if no other white person created similar conclusions, if the only person to form a negative opinion of blacks was myself—then my own opinion would be inconsequential. However, I can say with relative certainty that a very high percentage of the millions of whites living in this country at the minimum have created in their own mind stereotypes about blacks that generally are not positive and which they impute to all African Americans except for the few people who fit into their own narrowly defined qualifications for exceptions.

I have been one of millions, millions who may not be overtly racist or a significant risk to the physical safety of an African American. I have been one of millions. Think about it! When I think about it I'm staggered. How I would hate to have millions of people who have never had the opportunity to meet me or know me not like me, not want me around them, and not want to be around me. How blind I have been to think I have played no part in the deterioration of race relations in America. How wrong I have been to sit back on my couch in white suburban Chicago and point my finger at blacks universally, confident that I universally am innocent. My sin and my contribution to the racist environment that exists in America today have been both minor and of extreme importance.

But perhaps the most damaging part of a stereotype isn't the climate or culture that is created by the collective stereotypes of millions of people. Perhaps the most damaging aspect is how it affects our emotional reactions to tragedies and injustices committed against the stereotyped group.

When you have a presupposition that blacks are a violent people, it is not a difficult step, with every incident heard or seen about violence allegedly committed by an African American, to immediately conclude that the accused is guilty without ever giving the presumption of innocence until guilt is established.

When you have a presupposition that blacks universally abuse the welfare system, it's not a difficult step to refuse to help the truly needy in poor inner-city communities because of the abuse of others.

When you believe that blacks have a predisposition to self-destruct, it's not a difficult step to in disgust refuse to help an inner-city community rebuild after a riot has devastated it. It becomes easy to "wash our hands" of the matter and say, "You made your bed; now sleep in it!"

When you just generally don't like African Americans, it's easy to go along with or remain silent when your friends or family make racial slurs or disparaging comments about blacks.

When your whole thought process about African Americans has been structured around a negative stereotype, it's not such a difficult step to condone, brush aside, or explain away overt racism.

Just as we know an infectious illness left untreated could kill the infected person, the sin of stereotyping left unrepented can lead to the acceleration of overt racism and may eventually render reconciliation between our races not only unlikely but improbable and leave us wondering how and why violent racial conflicts have penetrated our cities, towns, and communities.

My friend, I am not persuaded nor is my conscience convicted that I as an individual white man am responsible for or guilty of all the past or present atrocities or injustices experienced by African Americans and their ancestors. I wish they had never happened, that a slave was never bought on American soil, that a Negro or colored person was never told to drink from a separate water fountain or to sit in the back of the bus. I am truly sorry that you and your parents and their parents back to the ancestor who was first enslaved—that you and they had to experience the atrocities and injustices that collectively you have had to experience at the hands of whites in America. In a way I wish I could apologize for all those wrongs, that you could forgive me for them, and that by my confession and your forgiveness that our two races could be reconciled. But I don't think that confession or apology is mine to make. Someone, somewhere, in a significant position of leadership in our country should make that confession and apology, in their official leadership capacity. But I am only responsible for my own sin and for the acts of those I have been given leadership authority over. I wish I could help heal the near debilitating wounds inflicted upon African Americans over the years—but I can't.

My friend, I apologize for acting in ignorance and creating a stereotype in my own mind and then defining an entire race with this stereotype. I ask your forgiveness for helping to create an environment and culture that makes daily life for African Americans more difficult and more of a struggle than it needs to be. Although I have not been overtly racist, I have been passively racist—I see this now; please forgive me. But most of all please forgive me for the many times I have remained silent when I should have spoken out and for the many times I joined in the disparaging comments of my friends and peers. Forgive me for assuming the worst instead of believing the best and for passing judgment on mere allegations alone.

BZ

Brent,

Your apology letter demonstrated self-examination at a level I have never seen before. Such self-analyzation also demonstrates your commitment to racial reconciliation. I commend you. I unconditionally accept and appreciate your apology. In fact I get choked up every time I read it. Thank you.

Having said this, let me tell you that I have never experienced nor felt any personal rejection, prejudice, or racist feelings from you. Our relationship has been one built on mutual respect and personal appreciation for one another. I believe that it is possible, however, for a relationship like ours to exist without the issue of race ever coming up. Such a relationship would probably be superficial to some degree because I think that interracial friendships have to address the issue of race at some juncture in order to progress to any significant level of depth and understanding. Because of this belief, I am happy that we are friends because we have deepened our relationship by taking the challenge and the risk to address such matters of the heart.

I have to tell you, Brent, that sometimes I do have reservations with such apologies from "white folks" on this issue of racial reconciliation. Sometimes I fear that whites will see their apology as the end and not the beginning. I do not feel this way about you because I know your desire regarding this issue and we have discussed this before. However, when I was at the Promise Keepers conference in Atlanta, Georgia, last month, the leader of the movement asked all the black pastors and other men of color to come to the front of the stadium. The white pastors hugged us and cheered for us. I received many apologies from many of my white brothers. But I also felt uncomfortable because they didn't do anything to me personally, so far as I know.

But then I began to see tears drip down the cheeks of many of these pastors apologizing. It was then that I realized this was for them, not for me. I needed to offer forgiveness because many of these men felt guilt and shame for what some of them may have done to contribute to the overall environment of racism in this country. At that point my heart was touched because I realized the importance of offering forgiveness and acceptance to those men who offered apologies and obvious remorse.

So then why the reservations on my part? Maybe my skeptical heart believes that stadium-sized remorse will not lead to shoe-leather repentance—a true changing of action. This is wrong of me. This attitude in my heart doesn't believe the best about my Christian brothers. This attitude within me has caused me grief because it seeks more than an apology. I want a change. I want "white folks" to do something, to fight for justice, to lobby for my cause—our cause, God's cause regarding reconciliation.

How can I balance out this feeling inside of me, Brent? Tell me in your opinion what the "white guy" is thinking when he apologizes. I know you can't speak for all whites, but give me some perspective on this issue so that I know how to accept apologies from my white brothers.

Finally, I want to apologize to you, Brent. I must apologize on behalf of those black brothers and sisters who have held on to bitterness and resentment and have breathed hatred, retaliation, and prejudice from the pulpit to the pew. Frankly I'm embarrassed by my black Christian brothers who preach the gospel of blackness and reverse racism from the platform that God has given them and I apologize to you, my brother. For all the times a black person has used the "race card" or falsely blamed a white person or the white establishment for their own personal failures or errors in judgment, I apologize. And personally, for the times I have not stood up in your defense to defy generalizations or racist comments about white people when I knew that such adjectives did not fairly represent all white people, I apologize.

Beyond my apology, I commit to you, my brother, that I will stomp out prejudice against whites wherever I have the power to do so. I will discuss issues of racism candidly and defy racism and discrimination when I see it. I will not allow the candid talk about the unjust society, the overt racist, nor underground bigotry to degenerate into a "let's blame all whites" campaign or a "let's get even" mentality. I am committed to educating whites and blacks about what God says regarding racism and our responsibility to "maintain the unity of the saints." I am just as committed to preaching against the sins of unforgiveness, bitterness, malice, slander, unrighteous anger, and the refusal to love as I am about preaching against the sin of racism.

This is my commitment to you and to God, my brother. I love you.

DA

David,

Let me start by saying that with regard to your personal apology, I thank you and I unconditionally accept. With respect to your apology on behalf of others, I thank you for the thought and the acknowledgment and even the embarrassment. However, I believe the guilt is not yours to bear nor the apology yours to give. You are no more responsible for apologizing for the hatred and prejudice of others than I am. The fact that you are black does not confer responsibility upon you for the actions or words of another. Nor are you as an African American Christian responsible for sin preached from the pulpits of other African American Christian pastors.

Your question of what is the average "white guy" thinking when he apologizes is a difficult question and I must confess I share your skeptical perceptions, a skepticism rooted in years of observation of Christians making Sunday morning or evangelistic rally confessions that do not translate into Monday-Saturday life change. Just as the litmus test for a person's acceptance of salvation is observable life change, the litmus test for repentance of racial sins is also observable life change. Such life change would be easily recognized if we lived in an integrated world. However, since all but a handful essentially live in a segregated world, the opportunity for observable life change is limited.

What are whites thinking? Their confession is probably genuine, although I doubt if all those confessing have truly examined themselves and their hearts to make the confession personal instead of general. Will there be observable life change in those confessing? In the majority of cases, my guess is probably not, not because their confession was a hoax but rather because the opportunities to demonstrate life change do not readily present themselves in the lives of most of those confessing. Secondly, I doubt that there will be life change simply because I doubt that most who are confessing have taken the time to examine the issues that face our two races, nor have they addressed their presuppositions or stereotypes about the other race through which all racial interaction is analyzed.

Promise Keepers is bringing the issue to the forefront of the thoughts of white Christian men across the country. My fear is that the ensuing confessions by whites are cognitive, not heartfelt. And that those that are heartfelt will seldom result in daily life change. Is your skepticism reasonable? We'll see once the vogue of racial reconciliation wanes. Am I assuming the worst rather than believing the best? Hopefully our skepticism is not an accurate discernment of the truth. Hopefully in a couple years we will have to repent of our skepticism because we will have been shown to be wrong.

BZ

Epilogue

A Note to the Reader from Brent

*D*uring the time of these letters I served with David and others on Bridgeway Community Church's board of trustees. Bridgeway was a start-up community at that time, struggling to build a solid core and financial viability. Now they are a strong and vibrant, culturally diverse congregation.

About the time these letters on racial reconciliation were winding down, the church's trustee board discerned that the time had come to implement elder leadership. Concurrently, back in Chicago, my professional career was taking a dramatic and positive turn resulting in a rapid and progressive expansion of my direct management responsibilities. The combination of these two factors led me to step down from active involvement in the financial leadership of Bridgeway.

I look back now on those days and remember fondly our quarterly board meetings. What a pleasure to serve alongside three African American and two white brothers in Christ—all who had the primary focus and purpose of responsibly managing the finances and governance of the people entrusted to the Bridgeway family.

I've asked myself many times since then what was it that provided the desire to look within myself to examine my thoughts and my opinions about racial issues? What made these issues critical enough in my life to devote hours to writing letters and days away from home traveling halfway across the country in pursuit of racial reconciliation? A friend, a genuine friend of another race! For me that friend was a black man who asked me to join him in a cause that was greater than either one of us. Our joint efforts together provided the impetus and opportunity for a genuine discussion on racial matters to occur. Our relationship and friendship was not focused on racism or racial issues alone. It was focused on service to our Lord.

Perhaps you have such a relationship, or perhaps you desire such a relationship with an individual who has experienced life from a racial perspective different than your own. If so, what is your next step in racial reconciliation? What is my next step? Some of us may need to examine our heart and mind to see if there is any sin that needs to be removed. Some may need to take the basic step of making acquaintances with a person of another race. Some may need to be more deliberate in deepening existing relationships. Others may be sensing the Holy Spirit moving them toward a specific action. Perhaps priorities need to be adjusted. Whatever that next step is, though, until our personal priorities are altered, making racial reconciliation critical and essential to us, life will continue to be business as usual.

David and I both firmly believe that racial reconciliation within the church in America will not be fully achieved through passionate evangelistic-type rallies, but rather will be achieved one person at a time—through genuine relationships. These relationships will not be easy. Success will require time and commitment. You have a choice. Although we believe God's desire is that all of His children of any race worship and serve Him together, you have a choice about the reality of this happening in your life and your community. David and I hope and pray that you choose to move forward in your journey toward racial reconciliation.

Appendix A

Study Questions and Suggestions

Self-analysis Questions

1. What is my attitude toward those who are different than me?

2. When I think about conversations I've had regarding other people groups (blacks, Asians, Hispanics, etc.), what comes to mind?

3. Did I make disparaging comments? Did I tacitly or verbally approve the negative things others said? Which of my actions reveal how I truly feel about people who are different from me?

4. Have I shared personal time with someone outside of my race within the last sixty days (for example, had dinner together, invited him or her to my home, gone shopping)? If not, why not?

5. Do I care enough about racial reconciliation to make it an essential priority in my life?

6. What is my next step toward experiencing relational connectedness with a person of another race?

Group Discussion Questions

1. Do you feel that you have ever been discriminated against because of your race? How so?

2. Do you have a personal (not professional) friend from another race? Who? How has this friendship developed?

3. If your answer to the preceding question is yes, have you and your friend discussed the issue of race? If yes, explain what was said. If no, consider bringing it up.

4. Do you harbor ill feelings, negative opinions, or resentment toward any racial group? Which group(s)?

5. If your answer to the preceding question is yes, what is the primary source of these negative feelings or views?

6. Have your negative feelings changed over time? How so?

7. What kind of experiences would most likely change these feelings?

8. For nonwhites: What do you think it is like to grow up white in America?

9. For nonwhites: How do you think white people feel about the state of racism in America today? Why?

10. For nonblacks: What do you think it is like to grow up black in America?

11. For nonblacks: How do you think black people feel about the state of racism in America today? Why?

12. On what issues do you disagree with the perspective of one or both of the authors of this book? Explain how you disagree.

13. What would be your reaction if a family of another race bought the house next to yours? Why would you react that way?

14. What would be your reaction if three families not of your race moved into your immediate neighborhood? Why would you react that way?

15. Assume you are in the position to hire a person to fill a job opening. Two people have interviewed for the position; both are equally educated, experienced, and qualified. One is white and one is African American. Whom would you hire? Why?

16. What question do you have that you wish was discussed in this book? Why is that question important to you?

Appendix A

Suggestions for Pursuing Racial Reconciliation

Here are ten specific efforts that can be made in the pursuit of racial reconciliation.

1. Have personal and small group Bible study on passages such as John 13:1–17; 17:1–26; 2 Corinthians 5:11–21; Galatians 2; Ephesians 2.

2. Proactively develop relationships with those who are different than you in your workplace, neighborhood, or community.

3. Become a learner and listener to the pain of others.

4. Search your own heart for racist or prejudiced attitudes and repent.

5. Speak up against racist speech, jokes, attitudes, and actions.

6. Read books on the issues of race and reconciliation.

7. Give a copy of this book to a friend of a different race and then discuss it.

8. Join a multicultural church so as to integrate your family with the family lives of others from different backgrounds.

9. Start a multicultural church.

10. Move into an integrated neighborhood.

Appendix B

Articles Cited in Letters

Blessed Are the Peacemakers

Moody, June 1994, 9

Somalia, Sudan, Bosnia, Rwanda—by the time this appears in print, the list of nations devastated by senseless internal conflict may have grown even longer. Call it civil war, genocide, or tribal conflict, the results are much the same.

As each new region erupts, we respond to the tragic news with shock and compassion. But as the weeks of fighting wear on into months and the rhetoric of negotiations is repeatedly drowned by gunfire, we may lapse into resignation and helplessness. Or worse, we may conclude that justice is being served. For years these people have been sowing seeds of mistrust, hatred, and injustice. Now they are reaping what they have sown.

If that's true, the implications for us are frightening.

The distance between our homes and such places as Bosnia isolates most of us from a sense of involvement—beyond perhaps a passing thought to "pray for those people."

As we react to news reports of ethnic hatred "there," it's easy to neglect the much more personal implications. For the problem is not restricted to obscure corners of the globe: It's here in our own country and in our own communities.

Ethnic violence, whether here or abroad, does not erupt overnight. It grows from years of hatred. Its seeds are passed from one generation to the next, in careless comments, in individual's choices to treat another not as an equal, but as something less.

Each day, news reports in our major cities list the death toll from yesterday's gang violence. One gang member shoots a rival gang member, perhaps in a turf war, perhaps in revenge. Elsewhere, a neighborhood resident is slain by a bullet meant for another gang member.

When warfare breaks out in Africa or Eastern Europe, we can expect a call for United Nations peacekeepers. But what can we, as individuals, do for the strife in our own communities? How can we take steps to reverse the pattern of disrespect, distrust, or hatred?

Last summer in *Moody*, pastor Raleigh Washington and Glen Kehrein of Circle Urban Ministries spoke eloquently of our scriptural mandate to break down the barriers that too easily divide people. For believers, they reminded us, "There is no Greek or Jew, circumcised or uncircumcised, barbarian, Scythian, slave or free, but Christ is all, and is in all" (Col. 3:11).

Our mission of reconciliation, they emphasized, must extend beyond believers from different cultures. For God has "reconciled us to himself through Christ and . . . committed to us the message of reconciliation. We are therefore Christ's ambassadors, as though God were making his appeal through us" (2 Cor. 5:18–20).

To begin, we must assess our attitude toward those who are different. "Get rid of all bitterness, rage and anger, brawling and slander, along with every form of malice," the apostle Paul instructs (Eph. 4:31). The next step is action: "Be kind and compassionate to one another, forgiving each other, just as in Christ God forgave you" (v. 32). As Christ reminded the Pharisees, the Lord calls us not to neglect "the more important matters of the law—justice, mercy and faithfulness" (Matt. 23:23).

The steps to treat one another justly need not be dramatic, but should encompass the events of our daily lives.

While Chicago's elevated commuter trains are not officially segregated, they might as well be. Most riders choose to sit with "their own people." Few ever make the effort to speak with their "neighbors" who ride the same train at the same time each day. Like an uneasy truce, the situation is tolerated, but not enjoyed. Yet even in this environment, a person motivated by Christ's love can begin to make a difference.

Every morning as his train approaches his stop, Jim, a Caucasian Christian, makes a point to walk to the end of the car to speak to Bill, an older man whose wife is ill. A younger man, whose clothing shows pride in his African heritage, usually sits nearby and gets off at the same stop. Over the past month, Jim has begun speaking to him as well. At first it was just about the weather or the train's erratic schedule. Last week, though, Jim learned he was an electrician—a topic in which they have some common interest. This morning, Jim spoke to him a little longer and learned his name.

Outgoing by nature, Jim nevertheless recognizes the need for careful, deliberate steps in building a relationship that crosses racial lines. "I'm taking it slow with him," he explains. But among the 40 people who ride that train car each day, Jim has decided to do something in the name of Jesus toward ethnic reconciliation.

One can only wonder and pray what would happen if all our communities—and the Sarajevos of our world—were filled with more believers like him.

Used by permission.

___

For Many Blacks, Simpson Case Is, Indeed, about Race

Clarence Page, *Chicago Tribune*, 6 July 1994, sec. I, p. 15

O. J. Simpson's "genial, race-neutral style went down easily with white audiences," *Newsweek* observed in its first cover story on murder allegations against the former football star.

I first experienced the remarkable ability of celebrityship to neutralize race a decade ago as a Chicago television reporter when I was sent to cover a political rally in a white neighborhood that had been the scene of several anti-black riots, including one in which the Rev. Martin Luther King Jr. was hit in the head with a brick.

As a black man, I was apprehensive about who I might run into there, particularly since it was 1983 and I was covering a rally of whites who were trying to stop Harold Washington's campaign to be Chicago's first black mayor.

Washington eventually made it and so, it turns out, did I. After I arrived with my camera crew, I was relieved to find that I was regarded with backslapping glee by the local folks. One woman even asked for my autograph.

Back at the TV studio where I worked, an older veteran of the business, who also happened to be white, observed with a sarcastic chuckle, "You're not black anymore, Clarence. You're on television now."

That was pretty funny, I thought, but at least one white journalist I know was offended by that story. Why, he asked, should I have been nervous about visiting a white neighborhood? Wasn't I stereotyping a whole group of white people for the offenses of a few?

Guilty. Just like some people get nervous at the sight of young black males on a lonely street, I get nervous in neighborhoods that have a reputation for lynch mobs. The moral: Race makes a difference in attitudes, whether we want to talk about it or not, so we might as well talk about it. The experience of racism's historical victims is quite different from that of its traditional beneficiaries. Blanket refusal to acknowledge that perspective, even in the name of color-blindness, is in itself a form of dehumanization, the end product of racism.

Celebrityship also dehumanizes, but in a different way. Even white racists loved O. J.—or, at least, the image of O. J. they carried around in their heads—at least until the day he was charged with the murder of his wife, Nicole Brown Simpson, and her waiter friend Ronald Goldman.

Color-neutral was the way "The Juice" wanted it. Like countless other black youths, he put his eggs into the basket of athletics, won the hearts of football and movie fans and purposely shunned the Afrocentric route taken by his friend Jim Brown, a fellow star of football, movies, and domestic abuse rap sheets.

Brown, who has worked closely with street gangs and black businesses, wanted to make a movement. O. J. wanted to make money. White America was happy to oblige as long as he worked as hard for middle-American consumer culture as he did for his football fans. Even his interracial marriage, once grounds for the downfall of boxer Jack Johnson, caused no noticeable problems for Simpson. Polite society in the post-'60s era does not make a large matter of such things. But if white people seemed to see the controversy in color-blind terms, blacks are just as eager to see it in terms fully conscious of color.

I have heard in person and on black radio talk shows various complaints about how Simpson "forgot where he came from," simply because he had a white wife, even though his visits and financial support of kids back in the San Francisco projects where he grew up are well known.

But I also hear in the same discussions a widespread resonating respect, however begrudging it sometimes may sound, for Simpson as a "brother" who "made it" the best way he could in a system and society that is often hostile to the interests of low-income black men. His ease in the white corporate and country-club world helped to confirm what blacks have been saying all along about our abilities to slip into America's mainstream, if the mainstream only would give us a chance.

The social investment many blacks made in O. J. Simpson's image may help explain racially-split polling results like those in a Gallup poll for CNN this week, which found that 68 percent of the whites said they believed reported charges against Simpson compared to only 24 percent of blacks. A similar racial split disagreed on whether Simpson could get a fair trial.

One black woman professor I know refuses to let her mostly white suburban college students discuss the O. J. Simpson case in class. She says she is tired of blacks being the canaries in the coal mine of social debates about sexual harassment (Clarence Thomas), date rape (Mike Tyson), child molestation (Michael Jackson) and now domestic violence. Why, she asks, don't white men of similar fame get similar attention?

She also wonders whether the television networks would be nearly as interested in the O. J. case if its prime suspect had been white or its victims black. So do I. As famous as Simpson may be, I find it hard to imagine his arraignment would be receiving live daily network coverage had he been accused of killing a BLACK wife and her BLACK waiter friend. Something about the Othello-like drama of a black sports hero murdering his lovely blonde wife elevates this case to greater newsworthiness than Amy Fisher, the Bobbitts and the Menendez brothers combined.

Having tried so hard to avoid acknowledging the differences race still makes in modern society, many people are surprised, even offended when the ugly topic persistently reemerges in the O. J. Simpson case. I, too, am disappointed. When the Simpson saga first broke, I was hoping we have come far enough as a nation to say the color of the characters in this story don't make a difference. Unfortunately, we have not come that far. Not yet.

Used by permission.

Southern Baptists Approve Apology for Longtime Racism

Washington Times, 21 June 1995, A3

The overwhelmingly white Southern Baptist Convention, born of the split between North and South over slavery, apologized to blacks yesterday for condoning racism for much of its history.

The vote in favor of the resolution received a standing ovation from the 20,000 members of the nation's largest Protestant denomination gathered for their annual convention.

The resolution denounces racism, repudiates "historic acts of evil such as slavery" and asks for forgiveness. It commits the 15.6-million-member church to the eradication of vestiges of racism and notes that the denomination failed to support the civil rights movement of the 1950s and 1960s.

The Rev. Gary L. Frost, the only black in the faith's leadership, accepted the apology on behalf of black Southern Baptists.

"We pray that the genuineness of your apology will be reflected in your attitude and your actions," said Mr. Frost, a pastor from Youngstown, Ohio. He and the denomination's president, the Rev. James B. Henry, embraced at the podium after the vote.

Supporters of the resolution hope it will open the door wider to evangelizing among blacks and other minorities. The convention has been making strides in that area by founding mostly black churches.

The Southern Baptist Convention was created in 1845 in a split with the American Baptist Convention over the question of whether slave owners could be missionaries. The church was silent or actively opposed civil rights through the 1970s, and many congregations excluded blacks. The denomination first declared racism a sin in 1989.

The apology resolution was approved overwhelmingly by a show of color-coded ballot cards after a few minutes of debate.

Several delegates said the measure would discredit the denomination's founders and its fair-minded members.

"It asks all Southern Baptists to apologize," said Dale Smith of Oxford, Ala. "Our convention, however, is made up of dear brothers . . . who took up arms against slavery."

"Certainly we do not ask anyone to join in confessing wrong of which you are not guilty," said the Rev. Charles Carter, chairman of the resolution committee. Referring to the 150th anniversary of the denomination's founding amid the slavery debate, he added, "This could be Southern Baptists' finest hour."

"I think it's an admirable resolution, and I would hope that it would not merely be a resolution that is on paper," said the Rev. Clifford Jones, president of the General Baptist Convention in North Carolina, a predominately black denomination. "To merely denounce historical racism and/or slavery and yet not actively seeking to promote parity, justice, and equality in the 21st century is really an act of futility."

About 1,800 of the 39,910 churches in the Southern Baptist Convention are primarily black, spokesman Herb Holinger said. He said there is no official count of black members.

Several of the 39 Southern Baptist state conventions have approved a version of the anti-racism resolution.

"I think it will go a long way toward uniting the convention at all levels," said the Rev. J. C. Rose of Lakeland, Fla., who is black.

Used by permission.

Southern Baptists Offer an Apology

USA Today, 21 June 1995

The Southern Baptist Convention on Tuesday repudiated slavery and racism and apologized to African-Americans for the denomination's segregationist past.

The overwhelming vote for an anti-racism resolution came at the group's convention in Atlanta. Leaders of the nation's largest Protestant denomination called the resolution a bold move to shed a racist image born when the group was founded 150 years ago in a show of support for slavery.

The vote was enthusiastic—but not unanimous.

In a debate lasting 12 minutes, several members spoke against the resolution, some objected to disavowing the group's founders.

"It asks all Southern Baptists to apologize," said dissenter Dale Smith of Oxford, Ala. "Our convention, however, is made up of dear brothers who took up arms against slavery."

"Naysayers, however, were in the minority," said President James Henry.

Charles Carter, pastor of Shades Mountain Baptist Church in Birmingham, said the resolution would not appease everyone. "For some people this resolution may say too little. For some, it may say too much," said Carter. "But hopefully we have expressed where the vast majority of our constituency is."

"I think it will go a long way toward uniting the convention at all levels," said the Rev. J. C. Rose of Lakeland, Fla.

The Southern Baptist Convention was formed in a schism with the American Baptist Convention in 1845 over whether slave owners could be missionaries. The group has grown to 15.6 million members in 40,000 churches. But membership among whites has been flat in recent years.

A version of the racial reconciliation resolution, seen as a way of opening the door to evangelizing among blacks and other ethnic groups was approved by eight state Baptist conventions last year.

About 1,600 predominately black churches are affiliated with the Southern Baptists. Many retain affiliation with one of several other Baptist denominations.

Carter, chairman of the convention's resolution committee said implementing the resolution would be the hardest task.

"Words such as we are trying to say here must be authenticated by action," said Carter, "Doing this today is far easier than it may be to implement it locally (in churches) and personally (in individual Christians)."

Henry, too, acknowledged a lack of church enforcement saying, "The Lord will have to do the implementation. In our church we cannot pass a law or make a church do anything because we're not autonomous."

"We have set a high-level watermark for us to move toward," he added.

Rufus Spain, author of *At Ease in Zion: A Social History of Southern Baptists*, doubted there would be "sweeping" changes in churches, even where the resolution is actively embraced.

"As recently as today many Southern Baptists think segregation is the way to go," he said. "Baptists historically reflect the views of society, whether it be segregation or slavery.

"I think it's a good PR move, but I don't think it'll go further than that."

Used by permission.

Suggested Reading

Cooper, Rodney L. *We Stand Together*. Chicago: Moody Press, 1995.

Evans, Anthony. *Let's Get to Know Each Other*. Nashville: Thomas Nelson, 1995.

Hacker, Andrew. *Two Nations: Black and White, Separate, Hostile, Unequal*. New York: Scribner's, 1992.

Pannell, William. *The Coming Race Wars?: A Cry for Reconciliation*. Grand Rapids: Zondervan, 1993.

Perkins, Spencer, and Chris Rice. *More Than Equals*. Downers Grove, Ill.: InterVarsity Press, 1993.

Schaeffer, Francis A. *The Church at the End of the Twentieth Century*. Downers Grove, Ill.: InterVarsity Press, 1970, 126–30.

Washington, Raleigh, and Glen Kehrein. *Breaking Down Walls*. Chicago: Moody Press, 1993.

West, Cornel. *Race Matters*. Boston: Beacon Press, 1993.

Rev. David Anderson is the founding and senior pastor of Bridgeway Community Church, a young multicultural congregation located in Columbia, Maryland. He is also the president of the Bridge Leader Network, a multicultural leadership consulting organization; and a part-time professor of cultural diversity and leadership management at the University of Phoenix. David received his bachelor's and master's degrees from Moody Bible Institute and is currently a doctoral candidate at Oxford Graduate School. On completing his undergraduate degree at Moody, David served as a pastoral intern at Willow Creek Community Church for two years, after which he planted Bridgeway Community Church with the help of a few core people. David has also served as the president of the Moody Bible Institute Alumni Board. David and his wife, Amber, have three children and make their home in Columbia.

Brent Zuercher is the Tax Director for the U.S. operations of a European-based manufacturing company that conducts business in 165 countries around the world. Brent's responsibilities include income and value based taxes for seven U.S. manufacturing and distribution companies with annual revenues of five hundred million dollars. Brent and his wife, Diane, have three children and reside in the Chicago suburbs. Brent is a CPA and received his undergraduate degree from Southwest Baptist University and his master's degree from DePaul University.